$\frac{3}{8}$

Principles of the Flute, Recorder and Oboe

PRINCIPLES OF THE FLUTE RECORDER & OBOE

By

Jacques Hotteterre le Romain

Translated & Edited by
David Lasocki

FREDERICK A. PRAEGER, *Publishers*

New York · Washington

BOOKS THAT MATTER

Published in the United States of America in 1968
by Frederick A. Praeger, Inc., Publishers
111 Fourth Avenue, New York, N.Y. 10003

Copyright 1968 in London, England, by David Lasocki

Library of Congress Catalog Card Number: 68–27615

Printed in Great Britain

Table of Contents

INTRODUCTION

Why should anyone living in the middle of the twentieth century wish to read a book about the principles of playing the flute, recorder and oboe written at the beginning of the eighteenth century? The answer is that our appreciation of old music is reaching the stage where we are no longer content to play it as if it were written for modern instruments and performing techniques, but are looking for ways of making it come alive, and finding that the surest method of doing this is to follow carefully the instructions handed down to us in the contemporary instrumental tutors. We are fortunate in that the men who wrote about musical matters— Hotteterre, Quantz, C. P. E. Bach—were those most qualified to do so. They had absorbed the musical performance of their time to an extent that only the top professionals can, and passed their skills on to others so that they too might share in the living musical experience. Music has altered radically since then, not only the content but also the way in which it was notated, and so our only means of finding out how it really sounded is to read these books, and then try to put their principles into practice ourselves. I am not suggesting that we can do this as successfully as the original readers could have done: our ears have heard things which they never heard, our taste has changed. But we must make the attempt; for this, as I know from my own experience, helps to breathe life into old music, and it becomes much more enjoyable, much more satisfying to experience.

Who, then, will read this book? The principal readers will of course be those recorder, flute and oboe players who wish to make this attempt to recreate the sound of old music. However, all those who are interested in this field should find something of use. As well as the specific technical instructions for the instruments which one expects, there are statements on the difficult subject of rhythmical inequality in French music, and the performance of both written and unwritten ornaments, which are important for a proper appreciation of the 'French style'. Some of the extra material which I have included in this introduction will also be of general value.

Although the one-keyed flute was given superior status to the recorder in the book, it is because of its interest to players of the latter instrument that it will principally be read. The recorder is such a well-known (yet at the same time little-known) instrument that the reasons for this will be obvious. Will there come a time when it is read again mainly for its value to players of the one-keyed flute? I sincerely hope so, but I doubt it. Modern flautists still play recorder music on their instruments, and are a long, long way from the stage of universal acceptance of playing old flute music on the flutes it was intended for. But, as we shall see later on, a little progress is being made along these lines. The baroque oboe is being played again[1] (although to a lesser extent than the baroque flute) and, of course, this book is of use in this respect.

Compared with a figure such as Quantz, the amount known about the life of Jacques Hotteterre le Romain is small. This is partly because he did not leave us an autobiography, and partly because he had a rather uneventful life, nearly all of which must have been spent in one place. However, even though the material is slight, is has been subject to a surprising number of errors, at the hands originally of nineteenth-century writers, but continued to this day by other writers who copied from them without taking pains to find out the truth. The biographical information given below is mainly taken from a book by Ernest Thoinan called *Les Hotteterre et les Chédville, célèbres joueurs et facteurs de flûtes, hautbois, bassons et musettes des XVIIe et XVIIIe siècles*, published in Paris in 1894. This cleared up most of the mistakes made over the names, dates and works of this family, but because it was only published in a limited edition (among other reasons), its newly established facts took a long time to be absorbed by writers on the flute.

---

[1] See for example Michel Piguet's record 'The Barock Oboe' (ORYX 710 and ODYSSEY 3216005o).

Biography

Jacques was probably born in Paris, where his father Martin married Marie Crespy; where he lived for a long time, and where he died about 1761. The year of his birth is not known, but is usually estimated to have been around 1680. The origin of his name 'le Romain' presumably lies in a stay he made in Rome early in his life, but there is no certain information on this point. Once he had returned to France he was admitted into the musicians of the *Grande Ecurie du Roy*[1] as bassoonist and gambist, succeeding his relative Jacques-Jean Hotteterre. This occurred between 1705 and 1707, for at this latter date he had already taken the title of 'Ordinaire de la musique du Roy'. Although the records say that he played the above mentioned instruments, he must have also been able to play the flute, and play it well, for the *Mémoirs de Frévoux* announcing the publication of this present work in 1707 remarked, 'The name of the author is a sufficient guarantee for the excellence of the work. This skilful flute-player is well acquainted with all the secrets of his art'.

His first big success was made with this flute tutor in 1707. It came at a good moment, for it was towards the end of the seventeenth century that the flute was introduced into French orchestras. H. Macaulay Fitzgibbon in an article, 'Of soft flutes and recorders'[2] says, 'The transverse flute was introduced into the Paris Opera House in 1690 by Jacques Hotteterre le Romain, a chamber musician to Louis XIV'. No sources are given for this information, which is understandable, seeing that Jacques was probably about ten at the time! Several other mistakes are made in this article. Hans-Peter Schmitz in his *Querflöte und Querflötenspiel in Deutschland während des Barockzeitalters* (p. 45) says that Lully introduced the flute into the orchestra for his opera *Isis* in 1677, when the flautists (who doubled on recorders) were Louis,

---

[1] 'The musicians of the Grande Ecurie, some of them on intimate terms with the king, were among the most privileged and famous in Europe. Many were composers, all played several instruments, and some were well-known instrument makers.' James MacGillivray in *Musical Instruments* (Penguin, Faber).

[2] *Musical Quarterly*, 1934, p. 222.

Jean, Nicolas and Jeannot Hotteterre. Thus Jacques's family was intimately connected with the early success of the instrument. Amateurs became smitten with it, and preferred it to the recorder. The tutor thus met a great need, as the success it achieved testifies. The numerous editions, translations and piratings are listed later.

You will notice that at the beginning of the tutor Jacques says he is 'preparing some suites of pieces composed expressly for the flute'. These followed in the next year (1708) under the title, *Pièces pour la flûte traversière et autres instruments, avec la basse continue. Livre Premier. Oeuvre Second.* There was a shortage of pieces for the flute at this time, and these were some of the first suites written in France for this combination (although de la Barre had already written pieces for unaccompanied flutes). The usual practice was to adapt violin music and songs. Michel Corrette's flute tutor[1] (p. 50) describes how violin music was adapted for the flute. The process consisted of transposing up an octave notes below *d'*, and occasionally others in order to preserve musical sense.

Jacques was very much sought after to give lessons. He often called his compositions by the names of his pupils—a shrewd business move which brought him wealth as well as fame, for his pupils were often of the aristocracy.

After many musical works in the intervening years (see later list), it was in 1719 that his second treatise appeared. This was called, *L'Art de Préluder sur la flûte traversière, sur la flûte à bec, sur le hautbois, et autres instruments de dessus,* and is recommended to readers of this present work as a complementary tutor. The volume carries the ancient privilege of the King, where he is described as, 'well-loved Jacques Hotteterre, one of the musicians of our chamber for the flute', and which finishes by saying, '. . . we permit the said Jacques Hotteterre le Romain to have the said work printed and engraved'. The repetition of this same privilege in several of his works, makes truly inexplicable the persistence on the part of many writers in calling him Louis.

Although Jacques was the descendent of an old and distinguished line of instrument makers, it is not certain whether he did make them himself. Thoinan supposed that Jacques was so busy playing

[1] *Méthode pour apprendre aisément à jouer de la flûte traversière* (Paris *c.* 1740).

and teaching the instrument that he did not have time to make any. However, Uffenbach (who made a musical tour of Europe between 1712 and 1716) says in describing a visit he made to Jacques in 1715, '[he] showed me many beautiful flutes which he himself makes'[1]. This seems to be the only piece of contemporary evidence on this point. A flute he is believed to have played is now in Berlin. It bears the name Hotteterre and the mark of an anchor, which belonged to his grandfather Jean and which might have been passed on to Martin and then to him. But it could have been made by his grandfather, in which case it must date from before 1678, the date of Jean's death.

Jacques married Elisabeth-Geneviève Charpentier, the daughter of a notary, and had several children including at least three sons—Antoine-Jacques and Jean-Babtiste who were also musicians, and Jacques-Louis, Parliamentary advocate. Only these last two survived their father.

Although the flute was Jacques's main instrument he did play bassoon and gamba as we saw above, and he was extremely skilful on the musette which he had been taught to play by his father. In 1737 he wrote a tutor for this instrument. He is less brief than in the flute tutor, and adds a number of musical pieces. In this work he describes himself as being the son of Martin Hotteterre and the grandson of Jean—which makes the calling of his father 'Henri' in several books quite inexcusable.

As well as being flute player to the chamber of the King, he retained all his life the post at the *Grande Ecurie*. Records tell that at one point he asked (and received) 6,000 pounds to keep this position.

I have called him by the sole name Jacques here, for this is the one given to him on his musical works. However, documents exist where he calls himself Jacques-Martin Hotteterre. *Grove V* records, '. . . son of Martin, after whose death he called himself Jacques-Martin' [Martin died in 1712], and Roger Cotte in *Die Musik in Geschichte und Gegenwart*, Vol. 6, p. 786, calls him Jacques Martin without a hyphen. Both these articles are based on Thoinan's book, and no other source of the extra name is given.

---

[1] See Eberhard Preussner: *Die Musikalischen Reisen des Herrn v. Uffenbach*, (Bärenreiter/Kassel 1949 p. 128).

The National Gallery in London has a picture[1] attributed to the painter Robert Tournières (1667-1752), which shows a gambist, three flautists and a standing figure gathered around a table, on which is some music by the flautist Michel de la Barre. Various authors say that two of these flautists are the brothers Jean and Jacques Hotteterre, although the National Gallery catalogue states that these allegations have no foundation. Despite this the picture is worth looking at,[2] and is interesting in that one of the flutes appears to have two extra finger holes which could not, in my opinion, have had any possible use.

Jacques Hotteterre le Romain died in 1760 or 1761, for his name no longer appears after this latter date in the estate of the household of the King.

The article by the famous nineteenth-century musicologist Fétis in his *Biographie Universelle des Musiciens*[3] seems to have been the main source of the mistakes made by later writers. His article starts, 'Louis Hotteterre, called "le Romain", third son of Henri, the most famous player of the flute in the second half of the seventeenth-century and the start of the following', and goes on from there! For his mistake over the date of the first edition of this book see the footnote on the title page.

Editions

The original edition was published in Paris by Christophe Ballard in 1707. There are copies of this in the British Museum and the Library of Congress in Washington. Alterations made in other editions have been given in the footnotes where they appear.

Reprints of this were done in 1713 (Library of Congress have a copy), 1720, 1722 (Library of Congress), and 1741. On the title page of the 1722 edition the publisher is now called J. B. Christophe Ballard. An edition with additions was made by Bailleux sometime after 1760—more than fifty years after the first one.

[1] Catalogue No. 2081.
[2] It is reproduced with my article, 'The baroque flute and its role today' in *Recorder and Music Magazine*, February 1967.
[3] 2nd edition, Paris 1883, Vol. 3, p. 373.

The *Encyclopédie* edited by Diderot and d'Alembert uses quotations and summaries from the work in its articles on the flute and recorder, first published in 1756. There are a few interesting changes in the textual quotations, which are noted in my footnotes when they occur. It is, however, unfair to dismiss these two articles as mere copies of Hotteterre. About half of each is devoted to original and important material, for instance that on the making of recorders.[1]

Fétis cites editions in Amsterdam in 1708, 1710 and n.d. The Library of Congress has a copy of one thought to date from 1708, pirated by Estienne Roger. The facsimile with German translation published in 1941 by Bärenreiter/Kassel is an undated Roger edition. The translator, H. J. Hellwig (who, incidentally, calls the author Louis and his father Henri and is very mixed up about dates) says that it was originally published in 1728, without giving any reasons for this dating.

There was an edition in Dutch in this year, under the title, *Grond-Beginselen Over de Behandeling van de Dwars-Fluit. In oen duidelyke Verhandeling over het recht gebruik, in een Korte Leeroeffening van dien vervat. Door Den Heer Hotteterre den Romein; Voornaame Muzik-Meester. Overgezezet* [translated] *door Abraham Moubach.* T'Amsterdam, van M[ichel] C[harles] le Cène, 1728. There is a copy in the Library of Congress.

There was an English translation of the flute part, the publication of which was announced by the London *Daily Post* on 25 October 1729. This was entitled, *The Rudiments or Principles of the German Flute, Explaining after an easy method everything necessary for a learner thereon to a greater nicety than has been ever taught before. Wrote in French by the Sieur Hotteterre le Romain; Musician in Ordinary to the late French King; and faithfully translated into English. To which is added A Collection of Familiar Airs for Examples.* London. Printed for and sold by I:Walsh sevt. to his Majesty at ye Harp and Hoboy in Catherine street in the Strand; and Joseph Hare at the Viol and Hoboy in Cornhill near the Royal Exchange. Price 2

[1] See my article 'Diderot on the Recorder', *Recorder and Music Magazine,* May 1967, and Eric Halfpenny's 'A French Commentary on Quantz' (*Music and Letters,* 1956, p. 61).

Shillings. There is a copy of this in the Library of Congress, which was formerly in the Dayton Miller Collection. Miller, in his *Catalogue of Books . . . relating to the flute,* says of it that, 'It consists of a complete translation of the treatise by Hotteterre . . . The *Modern Musick-Master* contains a pirated and incomplete translation . . . There is ample evidence that this book antedates the *Modern Musick-Master* and is the source of its text and of . . . . many later books . . . undoubtedly the earliest tutor in the English language.' The translation is, in fact, not quite complete.

The *Modern Musick-Master* which he mentions is now available in facsimile from Bärenreiter/Kassel, and the flute section is also available separately under the (original) title of *The Newest Method for Learners on the German Flute.* The work was first published in 1731, and also contains a section on the recorder, which, however, is not at all influenced by Hotteterre's tutor. The copyist was not very careful, and the work contains a number of mistakes, some of which I comment upon later in my foot-notes.

Another English work which contains portions of Hotteterre's work in what appears to be a new translation, is *The Compleat Tutor for the German Flute* (John Simpson, London, n.d.) which Edgar Hunt was kind enough to show me. This is similar to many other anonymous piratings dating well into the second half of the century.

Hotteterre and his work were well known in Germany. The earliest reference to the tutor appears to be that in Johann Mattheson's *Neu-eröffnetes Orchester* of 1713: 'Someone with the name Hotteterre in France has taken the trouble to write two or three little treatises . . . which an amateur will find a not unprofitable aid.' Hotteterre is mentioned as the author of the work in his entry in Johann Gottfried Walther's *Musikalisches Lexicon* of 1732. An abridged version with tables and frontispiece reproduced is found in Johann Eisel's *Musicus autodidactus oder der sich selbst informierende Musicus* of 1738. Quantz in his flute tutor mentions Hotteterre as the author of the work, and also as a famous player. It is important to realize that before the publication of Quantz's book in 1752, Hotteterre's was the only complete flute tutor available in Germany.

Publications

I now come on to a list of the rest of the works of Jacques Hotteterre. I have put after each one in brackets editions published today, because I think it is important to follow up the instructions given in this tutor by playing some of the author's own pieces. I do not guarantee that this is a complete list as I have only included editions which I have seen personally and can recommend.

(a) *Pièces pour la flûte traversière et autres instruments, avec la basse continue. Livre Premier. Oeuvre Second.* 1708 (copy British Museum). 2nd edition 1715 (copy University Library, Rostock).
Modern editions include:
(1) Suite in E minor for flute and b.c., edited by Hugo Ruf and published by Bärenreiter (BA 3316).
(2) 'Echos' transposed for treble recorder solo, edited by Walter Bergmann and published by Schott (Recorder Library 17).
(3) 'Duo le Fargis' and 'Rondeau le Champestre' transposed for two treble recorders, edited by Leonard Lefkovitch and published by Schott (Recorder Library 38).

(b) *Sonates en trio pour la flûte traversière et à bec, violin, hautbois, etc.* 1712, Oeuvre 3.

(c) *Première suite de pièces à flûtes.* 1712. Oeuvre 4.
[Modern edition transposed for treble recorders, published by XYZ of Amsterdam (641)].

(d) *Deuxième livre de pièces pour la flûte et autres instruments.* 1715 Oeuvre 5. [Suite in D for flute and b.c., edited by Gustav Scheck and Hugo Ruf, and published by Ricordi (SY638)].

(e) *Deuxième suite de pièces à deux dessus, pour les flûtes traversières, à bec, violes, etc.* 1717. Oeuvre 6.
[Modern edition transposed for treble recorders published by XYZ of Amsterdam (718)].

(f) *L'Art de Préluder sur la flûte traversière, sur la flûte à bec, sur le hautbois, et autres instruments de dessus.* 1719. Oeuvre 7.
[Modern edition edited by Michel Sanvoisin and published by Editions Aug. Zurfluh, Paris].

(g) *Troisième suite de pièces à deux dessus, pour les flûtes traversières, et à bec, hautbois, et musettes.* Oeuvre 8.

(h) *Concert du Rossignol.* Oeuvre 9.

(i) *Méthode pour la musette contenant les principes, par le moyen desquels on peut apprendre à jouer de cet instrument de soimême à défaut de maître* . . . 1737. Oeuvre 10.

(j) *Sonates à deux dessus, par le signor Roberto Valentino, Opera quinta, accommodées au goût de la flûte traversière par Hotteterre le Romain.* 1721

(k) *Sonates à deux dessus, par le signor Francisco Torelio, recueillies et accommodées au goût de la flûte traversière par Hotteterre le Romain.* 1723.

He also arranged some violin sonatas of Albinoni for the flute, and published a few other miscellaneous compositions.

Rhythmical Alteration

The problem of inequality in eighteenth century music is a very important one, and Hotteterre sheds some interesting light on the subject. As well as the information given in Chapter 8, this extra material from *L'Art de Préluder* (Chapter 11) is useful.

> Slow 4 time is marked with C. It is beaten to four, usually very slow, beats. The quavers are equal: the semiquavers are pointed, i.e. one long and one short. It suits preludes or first pieces of sonatas, Allemandes, Adagios, Fugues, etc.
>
> Barred C is marked with ₵. The quavers must be equal in regularity unless the composer dots them. Italians scarcely use it, except in what they call Tempo di Gavotta and Tempo di Cappella, or Tempo alla breve. In this last it is beaten to two quick beats. Its normal tempo is 4 quick beats or 2 slow beats.
>
> 2 time is marked by a simple 2. It is used in Marches, Bourrées, Gavottes, Rigaudons, Branles, Cotillons, etc. The quavers are pointed. It is unknown in Italian music. It is normally lively and staccato.

$\frac{3}{2}$ time. The crochets are pointed like the quavers in the others. It is used for Graves in sonatas, etc.

Simple triple time is marked with a 3 or sometimes $\frac{3}{4}$. The quavers are almost always pointed in French music. It is used for Passacailles, Chaconnes, Sarabandes, Italian style Courantes, Menuets, etc. When the quavers jump and/or are mixed with semiquavers, they are played equal. It is sometimes very fast and sometimes very slow.

$\frac{3}{8}$ time. This suits slow Airs, like Canaries, Passepieds, etc. The quavers are equal, and the semiquavers pointed. Its true speed is lively.

$\frac{6}{4}$ time. The quavers are pointed. You use it in Loures, Gigues, etc. You rarely see it in Italian music. Mostly it is lively.

$\frac{9}{8}$ time. The quavers are equal and the semiquavers pointed. It is used in sonatas, and above all in Gigues. It has only been used in France for some time.

$\frac{6}{8}$ time. The quavers are equal and the semiquavers pointed. It is particularly suitable for Gigues.

$\frac{12}{8}$ time. The quavers are equal, etc. It suits Gigues above all. Usage is fairly recent in France. You sometimes meet three quavers in a beat in C or ₵ time, which is equivalent to this.

$\frac{2}{4}$ time. The quavers are normally equal, and the semiquavers pointed. Some composers mark it $\frac{4}{8}$. It is really only a time signature of 4 quick beats cut into two.

The references to Italian music in the above apply to the way it was played in France at that time. As Italian music began to have more influence upon the French, Italian style movements were commonly found mixed with ones in the French style in French pieces.

The rules given by Michel Corrette[1] in his later flute tutor are similar to those of Hotteterre, but here are some extra ones:

The four-time C or ₵ is much in use in Italian music, as in the Allemande, Adagio, Presto and Allegro of sonatas and concertos. You must play the quavers equal, and point the semiquavers two by two. They are sometimes played

[1] *Méthode pour apprendre aisément à jouer de la Flûte traversière* (c. 1740), pp. 4–6.

equally in Allegros and Prestos of sonatas and concertos. The $\frac{2}{4}$ or $\frac{2}{8}$ is the two-time of the Italians. It is often used in the Allegro and Presto of sonatas and concertos. You must play the quavers equal, and point the semiquavers. They are also sometimes played equally in sonatas. The $\frac{9}{8}$ is rarely found in French music, but often in Italian music, as in Gigues, Allegros and Prestos. The quavers are taken equally, and the semiquavers must be pointed.

The $\frac{12}{8}$ is found in Italian, German, French and English music, in four-time Gigues. The quavers must be played equal, and the semiquavers pointed.

I think it is worth setting down the basic rules as to when to play the short note values unequally, so as to make really clear what Hotteterre is referring to.

In any time signature there are three main ways of playing the notes of the shortest time value. Firstly, the notes may all be played equally. This method is called *détacher* and is used in passages where there are many large leaps (especially arpeggio figures) and many notes on the same line. In passages which move by step this equality must be indicated by dots over the notes (note that this did not mean staccato) or by words such as *notes égales, détachez* or *martelées*.

Secondly the first note of each pair of notes may be played slightly longer than the second. This effect is known as *lourer* and is used in passages which move in steps or small leaps. The actual degree of inequality understood by the word 'slight' will vary according to the context. The shortest notes of *any* time signature may be slightly unequal unless they go very fast. In 2, 3 and $\frac{6}{4}$ the inequality is made rather greater. This *lourer* effect is referred to as 'pointing' by Hotteterre.

Thirdly in passages in which the first note of a pair has a dot affixed to it, the first note should be played *very much* elongated. This can be called *pointer* or *piquer*, but the terms *pointer, piquer, lourer*, etc. came to mean any sort of inequality.

In very quick tempi the notes have to be played equal, or virtually so.

Pronunciation

An important question is raised by Hotteterre's use of the syllable *Ru* for articulation, viz. what kind of R does he intend you to use? I am very grateful to Edgar Hunt for making me think about this matter. In his book *The Recorder and its Music*[1] he asks, 'What kind of sound is this Ru? The French R is surely closer to our K and G sounds than to our English R: and yet in the German Flute section of *The Modern Musick-Master* and *The Compleat Tutor for the German Flute*, both of which are free translations of Hotteterre, his tonguing examples are rendered by ttrtrt and ttr, etc.!' Some time after the appearance of this book, a lecturer in French at one of the colleges of London University wrote to him and pointed out that the French R at Hotteterre's time was not like the modern French R, but was done with the tongue. Thus it was quite logical for these English works to use R for articulation.

The proof which I am now going to cite comes from the *Manuel Phonétique du Français Parlé*[2] by the distinguished Danish phoneticist Kristoffer Nyrop.

In section 85 he says: 'This dental (apical) [r] . . . In normal French a uvula [R] has been substituted for it fairly recently. This is not to say that the traditional [r] has disappeared in the face of the other one; on the contrary, it still seems to have numerical superiority over it. It can be heard in the whole of the middle of France, in the countryside and in a lot of small towns. It is often heard on the stage, above all in "déclamation pathétique", and almost always in singing—the so-called "singer's r". But the uvula [R] dominates in Paris and in general in a lot of the towns of the North and West of France. It is more aristocratic than the other one, and belongs essentially to the pronunciation of cultivated society, which is why we consider it to be the normal form of the letter r in the French language. That the lingual-dental pronunciation used to be that of Parisian society is shown, above all, by the famous scene from the Philosophy lesson in *Le Bourgeois Gentilhomme* Act 2. Scene 4 [Molière, 1671], "And the r, by taking

[1] Herbert Jenkins, London 1962, p. 53.
[2] 8th edition revised and translated by Alf Lombard: Gyldendal 1963.

the tip of the tongue to the top of the palate, so that, being brushed by the air which leaves forcibly, it gives way to it, and always comes back to the same position, doing a kind of trill: Rra". We have there an excellent definition . . . We must, however, note in passing, that this description of the [r] pronounced at "the top of the palate" is, without doubt, an exageration, and you must not follow to the letter indications of the old phoneticists. But the [r] can be, and could have been, formed very high on the teeth-ridge.'

I thought it necessary to quote this passage because this question has been discussed by musicians in the field who have not sought out such evidence. I think also that evidence is really there in flute tutors as well, for note that Hotteterre calls his articulations 'tongue strokes'. Quantz also uses R for articulation purposes, and he says[1] 'You must seek to articulate the letter r very sharply. This has just the same effect in the ear as if you were using the simple tonguing *di*: but it does not seem like this to the one who is playing.' It seems to me that this passage must mean that he too wants the lingual-dental [r], and this is despite the fact that the German [R] was not like this. But we must remember that educated Germans spoke French—some even to the exclusion of German. Also Quantz studied for a time with the famous French flautist Buffardin in Dresden, and probably learned some articulation methods from him.

History of tu *and* ru

M. Agricola (*Musica instrumentalis deutsch*, 1528/45) used *diri diri* for semibreves, minims and semi-minims. Stress was on the first syllable in *diri* which is clear from the rhyme which he made on it:

> *Wiltu das dein Pfeiffen besteh,*
> *lern wol das diri diride.*

S. Ganassi (*Opera intitulata Fontegara*, 1535) used *tere tere* as one of

---

[1] *Versuch einer Anweisung die Flöte traversière zu spielen*, Chapter 6, section 2, paragraph 2.

his basic forms of tonguing, the stress again being on the first syllable.

M. Mersenne (*Harmonie Universelle,* Livre Cinquiesme des Instrumens à vent, Proposition XXIII, 1636) may be regarded as a transition between these two and Hotteterre. He used examples of three types: *tara tara* for trills; *tatararararara..* for some semi-quavers and dotted notes in the figure 𝄞 𝄞 𝄞 ; and *tataratarata*
. . . for the figure

ta ta   ra ra   ra

𝄞 𝄞 𝄞 𝄞 𝄞

ta ta   ra ta   ra ta   ra ta   ra ta ra ta •

In eighteenth-century France the syllables were mainly stressed iambically: *turu* = ◡ -. Hotteterre's tonguing examples are amplified in Freillon-Poncein's *La Véritable manière d'apprendre à jouer en perfection du hautbois, de la flûte et du flageolet* . . . Paris, 1700. As in Hotteterre, there are cases where the stressing becomes trochaic instead of iambic—principally on fast semiquavers, where the grouping *túrutúru* . . . is an early kind of double tonguing, having a similar function to Quantz's *did'll* for example.

The use of these tonguing syllables was abandoned by the French school of flautists from about 1735 onwards, but was passed on to the German school. Quantz modified the vowel sound and used *tiri* and *diri*: Tromlitz used *ta* and *ra.*

Joseph Bopp has kindly pointed out to me that *te* and *re* are used as articulation syllables by the modern French school of flute playing. See, for example, the flute tutor of Taffanel and Gaubert (*Méthode complète de flûte*) where they are used for dotted notes.

Articulation

The information which Hotteterre gives on articulation is rather difficult to understand for various reasons, and some extra explanations here should not come amiss. Professor Betty Bang of the University of Iowa has a series of books on eighteenth-century articulation in preparation which she was kind enough to let me see, and I whole-heartedly recommend them to those who wish to get a much better idea of the methods employed. The discussion which follows owes a lot to her, and I would like to acknowledge her help and encouragement.

The articulation syllables used by the French wind players were closely related to the performance of the *notes inégales*. The basis is the little word *turu*[1]. The *tu* must be pronounced sharply with the tongue close to, or actually touching the teeth. This gives a very characteristic sharpness to the articulation. The *ru* is pronounced with the tongue, near to the teeth, as outlined in the evidence quoted above. The letter *u* is more like the German *ü* than an English *u*, but the vowel sound does not seem to matter. The *ru* syllable should be accented—in length especially. This is why it is pronounced on the first of a (long-short) unequal pair of notes in the French style. The actual inequality in the French music was left very much to the taste of the performer. Sometimes it was only a slight stress given to the first note of the pair, and at other times the first note was played over-dotted. It depended upon the context. The articulation was always considered as *turu*[1], i.e. with *tu* first, and so at the start of any series of unequal pairs, the articulation would go *tuturuturu*.. This little word has been called a tongued-slur, which is appropriate, for the *tu* is bound to the *ru* across the beat.

Another articulation word was in use viz. *tu*[1]*ru*. This is normally very slightly short-long, but loud-soft. It gives the impression of the normal stressing given to strong and weak notes in the bar. It was used for some equal notes, and also as a sort of early double-tonguing for use in very fast passages. If you try the two words out you will find that it is much easier to pronounce *tu*[1]*ru* fast than *turu*[1]. There are occasions when *tu*[1]*ru* may be long-short as in the exceptional passages in 3 and 2 quoted by Hotteterre. Hotteterre uses it on equal notes in the examples of semiquavers on the same line and leaping; and in figures of the type: ⌊ ⌊⌡.

Here finally is a table showing the inequality and articulation appropriate to each note value in each time signature. Where there are two categories for a particular note value, (*a*) means when the notes move by step or by small leaps, and (*b*) means when the notes are on the same line, or move by large leaps—especially arpeggio figures.

Time signature	Note value		Inequality	Articulation
C	semibreves, minims, crochets, and quavers		equal	*tu*
	semiquavers	(a)	a little unequal	*turu*ˡ
		(b)	equal	*tu*ˡ*ru*
₵	semibreves, minims, crochets, and quavers		equal	*tu*
	semiquavers	(a)	a little unequal	*turu*ˡ
		(b)	equal	*tu*ˡ*ru*
2	minims and crochets		equal	*tu*
	quavers	(a)	unequal	*turu*ˡ
		(b)	equal	*tu*
$\frac{2}{4}$ or $\frac{4}{8}$	crochets and quavers		equal	*tu*
	semiquavers	(a)	a little unequal	*turu*ˡ
		(b)	equal	*tu*ˡ*ru*
$\frac{3}{2}$	semibreves and minims		equal	*tu*
	crochets	(a)	unequal	*turu*ˡ (exceptions)
		(b)	equal	*tu*ˡ*ru*
3 or $\frac{3}{4}$ (Inequality is only little in $\frac{3}{4}$).	minims and crochets		equal	*tu*
	quavers	(a)	unequal	*turu*ˡ
		(b)	equal	*tu*
	semiquavers	(a)	unequal	*turu*ˡ (exceptions)
		(b)	equal	*tu*ˡ*ru*
$\frac{3}{8}$	crochets and quavers		equal	*tu*
	semiquavers	(a)	a little unequal	*turu*ˡ
		(b)	equal	*tu*ˡ*ru*
$\frac{6}{4}$	semibreves, minims and crochets		equal	*tu*
	quavers	(a)	unequal	*turu*ˡ
		(b)	equal	*tu*
$\frac{6}{8}, \frac{9}{8}, \frac{12}{8}$	crochets and quavers		equal	*tu*
	semiquavers	(a)	a little unequal	*turu*ˡ
		(b)	equal	*tu*ˡ*ru*

Ornamentation

Hotteterre gives the following extra information on his ornaments in his introduction to *Pièces pour la flûte* . . . *Livre Premier*:

You should observe that it is necessary to make *flattements* on almost all long notes, and to do them (as well as *tremblements* and *battements*) slower or quicker according to the tempo and character of the piece.

That you must make a *coulement* in all descending intervals of thirds.

That you often do a *double cadence* when you ascend one note higher after a tremblement.

That you must do *tremblements* on almost all accidental sharps[1] except when they come on very short notes, such as quavers and semiquavers.

You can scarcely determine all the places where the *accent* must be placed. You do it normally at the end of a dotted crochet when it is followed by a quaver at the same pitch (in time signatures where the quavers are equal). You do them on certain long notes, but you must use them rarely.

In some of his works Hotteterre makes use of these extra ornaments:

Instruments

Hotteterre does not give any account of how the instruments were made, so I refer you to the article on the recorder in Diderot's *Encyclopédie*.[2] Diderot's article on the flute mentions many sizes of flute apart from the usual one with *d'* as the lowest note. It is interesting that Hotteterre only mentions the normal size. It is

---

[1] Leonard Lefkovitch in his notes to Hotteterre's 'Duo and Rondeau' says that this refers to the notational convention of the time in omitting the sharpened leading note from the key signature, and inserting it in the body of the music when necessary.

[2] See my article 'Diderot on the Recorder', *Recorder and Music Magazine*, May 1967.

surprising that he does not mention any other sizes of recorder apart from the treble. From his preface it seems that he regarded the recorder as a dying instrument (in France), and, as he had really added it as an afterthought to his flute tutor, he presumably decided that there was no point in mentioning the other sizes which were less in use even than the treble.

For the benefit of the many recorder players who do not know anything of the one-keyed flute or its history, I will give here a brief outline. The flute of the Renaissance period was simply a cylinder with six finger holes and a mouth hole bored in it. Intonation is a little difficult, and it is impossible to play the notes *d* sharp. However, the tone is pleasing and I am glad to see that it is being played a little today. This was the kind of flute which took part in consort music which recorder players will know well.

Somewhere around the middle of the seventeenth century, probably in France, this instrument was converted into one made in three joints—just like the baroque recorder, which was improved in the same way at the same time—and a key was added to enable the *d* sharps to be played. This is the instrument shown in the frontispiece in this tutor—the kind of flute used by Hotteterre and his contemporaries. The overall shape was now a cone, sloping the opposite way to the oboe, and other differences were that intonation was much better, if still difficult, and that the tone was more colourful. One thing which especially made it worth reviving today is that the cross-fingered notes have a different tone quality from the others—something which is noticeable on the recorder to a much smaller extent. This gives most passages a completely different 'shape' to that given them by a modern Boehm flute.

Probably in the 1720s this flute was changed slightly. The middle section was split into two pieces, as Corrette describes in his flute tutor (p. 7): 'The most fashionable flutes are made in four pieces, so that they can be carried in the pocket more easily. All flutes are at the Opera pitch. But as when playing concertos you sometimes find that the harpsichord is too high or too low, you normally have several *corps de rechanges* of different lengths, to tune to the pitch of the harpsichord. This changing is only for the first [i.e. upper-middle] piece'. Up to three-quarters of a tone change could be made by this means. I do not know why the recorder was never improved in this way. Probably it was declining when the change was made on the flute, and therefore remained in the three-piece form we know today.

This flute was then the fairly familiar flute of the eighteenth century, which lasted up to about 1800, and which is now undergoing a revival for playing old flute music. Two pre-eminent modern players will be well known to recorder players. They are Hans-Martin Linde of Basel, and Gustav Scheck of Berlin. They have made many gramophone records using the instrument, and to gain an idea of how flute music really sounded in this era I recommend listening to some of these.[1]

For an account of the baroque oboe and its development from the shawm see James MacGillivray's chapter 'The Woodwind' in *Musical Instruments Through the Ages*, (ed. Baines), Penguin/Faber.

Sources

This translation was made from the copy of the first edition belonging to the British Museum (Catalogue No C. 119. e.1). Hotteterre's prose style is workmanlike, even awkward, and the tutor has been rendered fairly literally into English. It is hoped that this will retain some of the flavour of the original.

Acknowledgments

I would like to acknowledge the help I have had in editing this book from the following people: Edgar Hunt, my teacher for the one-keyed flute and recorder, who lent me a number of useful books, and suggested a number of ideas; Betty Bang, (the American flautist), who first showed me by her wonderful playing, that it is so much better to play eighteenth century music on the one-keyed flute in the ways recommended by Hotteterre and others, than to play it on the modern Boehm flute in the 'modern' way, and has

[1] Readers interested in the problems faced by those wishing to play the baroque flute will find them discussed in my article 'The Baroque Flute and Its Role Today', *Recorder and Music Magazine*, February 1967. This also contains a discography and list of replica makers.

helped me enormously with the articulation chapter; J. M. Thomson; Walter Bergmann; Peter Jüngst, who helped me with German translations; Anthony Lister who helped me to obtain photocopies and information on the old French [r]; the British Museum; and finally my family and friends who put up with my incessant talking about Hotteterre and his tutor very patiently!

DAVID LASOCKI
London

PRINCIPES
DE LA
FLUTE TRAVERSIERE,
OU FLUTE D'ALLEMAGNE.
DE LA FLUTE A BEC,
OU FLUTE DOUCE,
ET DU HAUT-BOIS,

Diviſez par Traitez.

Par le Sieur HOTTETERRE-*le-Romain, ordinaire de la Muſique du Roy.*

À PARIS,

Chez CHRISTOPHE BALLARD, ſeul Imprimeur du Roy pour la Muſique, ruë S. Jean de Beauvais, au Mont-Parnaſſe.

———————

M. DCCVII.

Avec Privilege de Sa Majeſté.

PRINCIPLES OF
THE FLUTE, RECORDER
AND OBOE

Divided into treatises

By *Jacques* HOTTETERRE *le Romain*
Chamber Musician to the King

PARIS
CHRISTOPHE BALLARD
sole printer of music to the King;
Rue St. Jean de Beauvais
in Montparnasse

1707[1]
With the privilege of the King

[1] Fétis thought that this was only a second edition, citing as evidence a catalogue of musical pieces at the back of *Méthode de Théorbe* by Michel-Ange, published in 1699, where the tutor is mentioned. However, not only was the author called Angelo Michele Bartolmi and the title of the book, *Table pour apprendre facilement à toucher le Théorbe*, but it was published in 1669! The catalogue had been added to the copy seen by Fétis at a much later date.

    If more proof than the date above were needed, the plates are also dated 1707. Moreover Jacques writes in the *Avertissement* to his *Pièces pour la flûte* . . . *Livre Premier* dated 1708, that 'Here are the pieces which I promised in the treatise on the flute which I had printed last year'.

PREFACE

As the flute is one of the most pleasant and one of the most fashionable[1] instruments, I believed I must attempt this little work, in order to assist the efforts of those who aspire to play it. I venture to flatter myself that my work will not be completely unworthy of the attention of those who have good taste[2] on this instrument, since my principal aim is to smooth the first difficulties, which usually give the most trouble. You could thus teach yourself the principles of flute playing with the help of this treatise. I have given demonstrations of how to do all the notes—naturals, sharps and flats; along with explanations of the way in which they must be adjusted. I also teach how you must do all the *tremblements* on these same notes; and then what are the ornaments necessary for playing correctly and with good taste. These rules and demonstrations could even make up for the absence of teachers, for some people have a natural ability for playing this instrument; and for them only the knowledge of the principles is lacking. You will also find a treatise on the recorder; as well as a comparison of the flute and the oboe, which could be used as a method for learning to play this latter instrument. I do not discuss the value of notes, or metre here. These are things which belong rather to a treatise on music, than to a treatise on the flute.

Those who believe that they need examples for putting into practice the instructions contained in this book, can obtain some

[1] Roger Cotte in his article on Hotteterre in *Die Musik in Geschichte und Gegenwart* (Vol. 6, p. 786) remarks, 'It is certain that he brought his instrument into fashion, and by this gave the recorder a decisive blow. In the France of this epoque it sank to the rank of an elementary instrument for beginners and amateurs.'
[2] The *Encyclopédie* of Diderot defines good taste as 'the ability to distinguish in works of art that which must please sensitive souls, and not injure them'.

from me which have the ornaments already marked in. For those who are more advanced, I am preparing some suites of pieces composed expressly for the flute.[1] You can also practise on *Brunettes*, and the Duos and Trios by the late Monsieur Gaultier of Marseilles, which have just been published.[2]

---

[1] *Pièces pour la flûte traversière et autres instruments, avec la basse continue. Livre Premier. Oeuvre Second.* Paris, 1708. See my introduction for pieces from this work published today.

[2] In the edition of 1722 he advises study of 'les Brunettes, les Parodies, les Tendresses Bacchiques, et la Clef des Chansonniers'.

Pierre Gaultier of Marseilles died in 1697. A book of trios was published posthumously by Ballard. Editions du Siècle Musical of Geneva publish a suite in G for treble recorder and bass continuo from this. Few ornaments are marked, and the reader should find it good material for practice of the principles of ornamentation set out by Hotteterre.

TREATISE ON THE FLUTE

Chapter 1

On the situation of the body and the position of the hands

As it is necessary to add grace to skill as far as possible in order to attain perfection in the practice in which you want to succeed, I will begin this treatise with an explanation of the posture you must assume when playing the flute.

Whether you play standing or seated, you must hold your body erect, your head somewhat raised and turned a little towards your left shoulder, your hands high but without raising your elbows or shoulders, your left wrist bent inwards[1], and your left arm close to your body.

If you are standing you must stand firm with your left foot forward, the weight of your body resting on your right hip; all without any constraint. You must, above all, be careful not to make any movement of your body or head, as some people do when beating time. This highly valued attitude is extremely gracious, and engages the eyes no less than the sound of the instrument pleasantly caresses the ear.

Regarding the position of your hands, you can see a picture of this above, which will be more instructive than everything I could write on this subject.[2] You should learn from this picture that you must put your left hand (A) on top; hold the flute between your thumb and first finger (B); bend your wrist underneath; and

---

[1] Diderot changes this to 'turned outwards'.

[2] Ernest Thoinan remarks (p. 39): 'The editions of Paris carry as frontispiece a flute player, whose fingers placed on the instrument are marked with letters, to which the explanation of fingering given in the first chapter refers. This engraving is by Bernard Picart, and passed generally for the portrait of Jacques Hotteterre. Although there is no certain proof on this count, the thing seems very likely, for our flautist is dressed in a large curly wig, and the costume which the King's musicians wore in this era. Could it be then, that the author of the tutor, wanting to give a perfect example, posed for the artist himself?'

arrange your fingers such that the first and second are curved a little, and the third is more stretched out.

As regards your right hand (C), you must hold your fingers almost straight; your wrist bent inwards a little; your thumb[1] opposite the finger on the 4th hole, or a little lower, and your little finger placed on the flute between the 6th hole and the moulding of the foot.[2] (You can see all this demonstrated in the picture). It is necessary to hold the flute almost straight, but lowered towards the foot (D) a little.[3]

[1] Diderot adds, 'which is turned out a little'.
[2] Corrette says that the little finger should always nearly touch the key, i.e. hover in the air just over the key.
[3] Note that the flautist in the picture has his flute lowered too much! This may have been due to the artist's desire to fit the flute in the picture, and still retain a balanced composition. Hotteterre does not say that you can see *this* point demonstrated in the picture!

Chapter 2

On the embouchure

Although many people are of the opinion that the embouchure cannot be taught by rules, there *are* some rules which will be extremely helpful for you in finding out how to do it. The advice of a good teacher to supplement the demonstration can save much time and trouble to those who wish to acquire this embouchure.

I will therefore both advise and demonstrate, as far as is possible on paper. You can see the demonstration in the picture at the beginning of the book.

Regarding the advice, it will not be more difficult for me to write it than to give it orally, and I will do it as intelligibly as I possibly can. You will know from the demonstration the way in which you must dispose your lips. It is necessary that you put them together, one against the other, except in the middle, where you must form a little opening[1] for the passage of the air. You do not push them forward,[2] but draw them back towards the corners of your mouth, so that they are smooth and flattened. You must place the mouth hole of the flute opposite this little opening; blow moderately, supporting the flute against your lips; and turn it inwards and outwards until you have found the correct position.

In order to observe all the rules, a precaution which will be of great help is to place yourself in front of a mirror. It is not necessary at first to think of placing any fingers, but only to blow into the mouth hole with all the finger holes open, and try to bring out a good tone. Afterwards you should place the fingers of the top hand in order; staying on each note, and blowing several times so

[1] Diderot adds, 'about one twenty-fourth of an inch high, and one third or one quarter of an inch long.'
[2] Diderot adds, 'as when you blow a candle to put it out'.

as to be quite sure of it: after which you should place the fingers of the bottom hand in the same order as those above. Beginners should not persist for too long in trying to do the first note *d'* which is completely stopped: because it can only be done by stopping all the holes perfectly; which is more difficult than you would think, but can be attained with a little practice.

When you have succeeded in getting a good tone out of the flute, you can start to learn the notes. For this you should look at the first plate of tones and semitones, and read the next chapter.

It is not necessary to observe exactly the rules which I have prescribed for the embouchure and for the position of the hands; but only in as much as you should not do something totally contrary to them.[1] For example, if a person should find that it is more difficult for him to blow the flute by smoothing and flattening his lips, than by pushing them upwards, because of the way his lips are made: then it would only be necessary for him to take those of my rules which are not contrary to this formation. You must always follow what seems most natural. It is the same with regard to the hands. There are some people who place the top one in a different way from how I have shown it, i.e. who hold the wrist outwards (making an arc), and support the flute on the end of the thumb. This hand position does not stop you from playing well, but it is not as natural nor as gracious as the other one: and besides, the flute is not as well supported. There are others who, not having been shown the principles, put their right hand on top and their left below, and hold the flute to the left.[2] I will not absolutely condemn this position of the hands, since you can play as well in this way as in the other, and there would be difficulties in trying to change it. But those who have not yet contracted this bad habit must take care not to fall into it.

[1] For example Corrette says, 'There are people who can only sound the flute by advancing the lower lip on the edge of the hole', but that this is permitted so long as the tone produced is pure.

[2] Michel Blavet (1700-68), the most famous French flautist of the generation after Jacques Hotteterre, played left-handed like this. The practice was fairly common, in fact, as it is just as easy to play a one-keyed flute in this way, moving the foot-joint round a little.

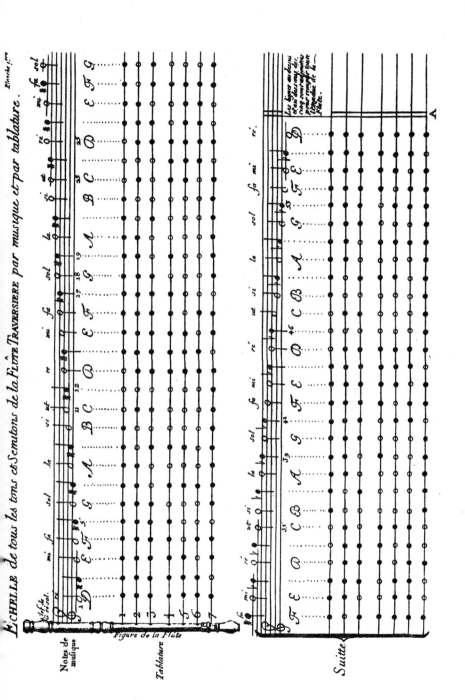

ÉCHELLE de tous les tons et Semitons de la Flute Traversiere par musique et par tablature.

Planche 1re

Notes de musique

Figure de la Flute

Tablature

Suitte.

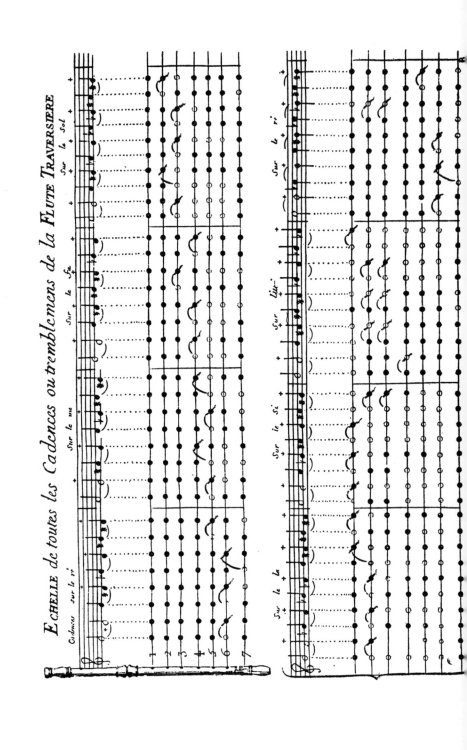

ECHELLE de toutes les Cadences ou tremblemens de la FLUTE TRAVERSIERE

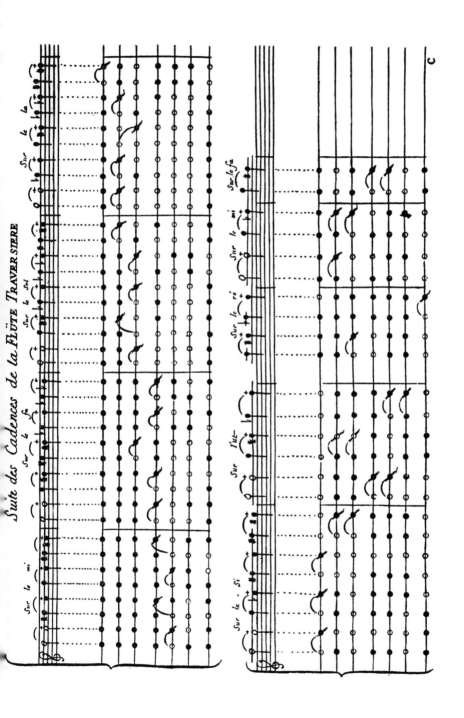

Suite des Cadences de la Flûte Traversiere

C

Chapter 3

First explanation of the first plate (naturals)

This plate represents two principal things:

(1) The notes of music at the top of the plate, shown on the five parallel lines, and distinguished by the names, Re, Mi, Fa, etc., and by D, E, F, etc. I have put these names in two ways for the convenience of foreigners, who normally use letters.

The G or French Violin Clef which you can see at the beginning of these five lines, is the one most used for flute music. It gives its name to the first line, on which it is placed,[1] and it is from this that you can find the place of all the notes, the order of which is observed in this demonstration.

(2) It contains a table which serves to explain the way of doing each of these notes on the flute, by stopping more or fewer holes. This table is demonstrated by the seven parallel lines, which correspond to the seven holes of the flute.

You can see on each of these lines a number of black and white circles, by which you know whether the hole which corresponds to each of the lines must be open or closed, in order to do such and such a note.[2] You can readily understand that the black circles represent the holes which must be closed, and the white ones those

---

[1] The Amsterdam edition of Roger used for the facsimile mentioned earlier, has here, in both cases, 'second line', and changes to the treble clef (for which this change would be appropriate) in the examples in the text: but sticks to the French Violin Clef in the fingering charts, to which *this* wording applies!
[2] This tutor differs from the many *Companions* and *Flute Masters* which appeared in England in this era, for they stuck to the dash notation borrowed from flageolet tutors. It is significant that the German flute section of the *Modern Musick-Master*, which is, as I have noted previously, mainly a translation of Hotteterre, inherits his notation: whereas the recorder section of the work, which is not influenced by Hotteterre, sticks to the dash notation.

which must be open. For example, below the first note, which is
d', you see seven black circles on the perpendicular line described
by the black dots. It is easy to understand that this represents the
seven holes of the flute stopped—the first six with the fingers, and
the 7th stopped with the key; which gives this note. You should
proceed in the same way for all the others, as I explain them
afterwards in greater detail.

From this plate you can thus discover the whole compass of the
flute, i.e. all the notes—naturals, sharps and flats. This compass
consists of two octaves and some notes.[1] The first octave contains the 1st note to the 13th. The second octave includes from the
13th note up to the 25th. This second octave is almost the same as
the first as far as the position of the fingers is concerned: only the
way of blowing the flute is different, apart from some changes of
fingers on certain notes, as you see demonstrated in the table. I
have distinguished the naturals with minims, and the sharps and
flats with crochets. I have done this to avoid too much difficulty at
first, for those who are not at all familiar with the groundwork.
They should content themselves with the naturals, without regard
for the others until they are more advanced.[2] It is necessary to
note that you must blow only gently in doing the low notes[3]:
and that you must stop well all the holes marked in the table with
black circles.

You thus know how the note *d'* must be produced, by the
seven black circles which are below it, as I have just explained.

After this note you should pass on to *e'* natural, which is the
3rd note, and which is produced by unstopping the 6th hole—as

1 The compass was extended fairly soon from *g'''* to *a'''* (e.g. see the Partita
for solo flute, BMV 1013, by J. S. Bach, first movement).
2 Corrette advises that you start with the naturals, but with c sharp instead of
natural, because 'that teaches the ear true modulation', seeing that, 'c sharp
is the leading note of the key of d'.
3 This is contrary to the rules of Quantz who says (Chapter 4, par. 21), 'You
must note especially that the notes in the low octave must be played more
strongly than those in the high octave all the time'. There appear to have been
two different schools of thought in flute playing with regard to tone. The
Quantz 'school' got a tone more like that of the modern flute, by methods
such as this, and differences in the structure of their flutes. Hotteterre would
seem to have belonged to the other 'school'.

you understand by the open O (which I also call white circle), which is on the 6th line of the table. You must give a tongue stroke to each note, i.e. articulate your breath as if you were pronouncing the syllable *tu* sharply.

f' is produced by unstopping the 5th hole, and restopping the 6th. This note needs to be adjusted with the embouchure by turning the flute inwards, to flatten it: because it is naturally a little high, seeing that the sharp is made on the same hole, as we will see in the explanation of the sharps and flats. You must remember to put your little finger between the 6th hole and the moulding of the foot, as I observed in the second chapter.

g' is made by lifting all the fingers of the bottom hand, leaving the little finger in the position which I have just indicated. This little finger must always remain in this place unless it is necessary to touch it on the key. You must be careful from the start not to raise your fingers a lot, and to let them fall plumb on the holes. As you have been obliged to turn the mouth hole of the flute inwards for *f'* you must replace it in its first position for *g'*.

a' by unstopping the 3rd hole. It is then necessary to put the 6th finger between the 5th and 6th holes which only serves (as does the situation of the little finger) to hold the flute in position, but which is nevertheless important for the freedom of the fingers. You must augment your breath, little by little, in proportion as you ascend.

b' by unstopping the 2nd hole.

c'' by unstopping the 1st and restopping the 2nd and 3rd.

d'' by stopping all the holes except the 1st. You must then augment your breath, so that the sound is sharp: though you must not do this too much, for fear that by blowing too strongly, you will climb an octave higher than necessary.

e'' by unstopping the 6th hole, by restopping the 1st, and by continuing to sustain your breath somewhat firmly, just as on the following notes.

f'' by unstopping the 5th hole, and restopping the 6th. It is again necessary on this note to turn the mouth hole of the flute inwards.

g'' by unstopping the 4th and 6th holes, without changing

anything else. You must replace the mouth hole in its normal position for this note.

I must note here for the benefit of beginners, that as they ascend on this instrument they will find the embouchure more difficult. So to soften the high notes, and form them more easily, they must take care to press their lips together more and more; to draw them back to the corners of their mouths; to push their tongue forward towards their lips; and to augment their breath little by little.[1]

a″ by unstopping the 3rd hole and by continuing to sustain your breath.

b″ by unstopping the 2nd hole.

c‴ by unstopping the 1st hole and restopping the 2nd, 4th and 5th.

This note is a bit delicate to adjust, for there are some flutes where it is high, and others where it is low. The expedient which you can adopt to lower it, is to blow more softly, and turn the flute inwards. If that is not sufficient, it is necessary to half stop the 6th hole without changing anything else: or to do it as I have demonstrated in the table (35th note). If, on the contrary, you notice that this note is too low when doing it in the first way I have explained; then you should only stop the 3rd, 5th and 6th holes.

d‴ by stopping all the holes except the 1st. You must force your breath a little, and press your lips together.

e‴ by unstopping the 3rd, 4th and 7th holes, and by stopping all the others.

Notice that the 7th hole is unstopped by leaning the little finger on the key. You must continue to force your breath.

Forced notes

The notes above *e‴* are forced notes, and cannot enter naturally

[1] These actions compensate for the earlier directive to 'augment your breath, little by little, in proportion as you ascend'. It looks at first as if Hotteterre had the idea that the second and third octaves are made only by blowing harder. But this passage shows that he wanted to express the right thing. All these are methods to make the diameter of the air lamina smaller, and raise the speed of the air current, with the same, or smaller, breath strength. Diderot omits these qualifying remarks, and is corrected in the article in the supplement of 1777.

in any piece. However, as you sometimes find them in Preludes,[1] I will put here those I could discover. Furthermore you must not persist in wanting to find them at the beginning, as it is a trouble which you must spare yourself until you are very advanced. It will be the same during the first days with regard to not going higher than *g''*, unless you have found the embouchure very easy. Then you could ascend higher, but with discretion, otherwise this would give you a lot of trouble to little purpose. It is absolutely necessary to start by forming the low notes well before doing the others.

f''' natural can almost never be done on the flute.[2] I have, however, found it on some flutes in the way I am going to explain. But you must not expect to find it indifferently on all kinds of flutes, or the *tremblements* which proceed from it: for this would be impossible. It is produced by stopping fully the 1st, 2nd and 4th holes, by stopping the 5th half way, by unstopping the 3rd, 6th and 7th, and by blowing very sharply. Furthermore, I have not shown it in my first plate, because it is not really a note on which you can count.

f''' sharp can be reached more easily. You must stop all the holes except the 2nd.

g''' by stopping the 1st and 3rd holes, and unstopping all the others.

You could find several further notes above these, but they are so forced, and so little use, that I advise people not to take the trouble to attempt them.

---

[1] e.g. in Hotteterre's own. Corrette later says that *g'''* sharp and *a'''* are 'scarcely used, except in preluding', thus carrying on this tradition of using very high notes in preludes.
[2] Handel uses *f'''* in his flute sonata Opus 1b, published in 1722 (?) (and written rather earlier): and this note is commonly found later on in the century. Quantz, who gives the compass of the flute up to *a'''*, never himself played above *e'''*, according to Tromlitz in *Über den schönen Ton auf der Flöte*, Leipzig, 1800: and Quantz himself says (Chapter 4, par. 20), 'The highest usable note that you can invariably produce is *e'''*. Those which are higher require a particularly good embouchure'.

Chapter 4

First explanation of the second plate
(tremblements *on naturals*)

Now that I have run through the naturals, I am going to discuss
the *tremblements* or *cadences* on these same notes, and I am going to
present all the examples of them, which are also marked in a table
in the second plate. I have put all the tones and semitones together
just as in the first plate. But I will only run through the *tremblements*
on the naturals at first, as I have already dealt with these notes
themselves. You will see them distinguished by minims in the same
way as before.

In order to convey what a *tremblement* is to those who have no
idea, it can be defined: 'An agitation of two notes a tone or semitone apart, and beaten several times in succession. It is begun on
the higher note, and finished on the lower; articulation only being
given to the first, for the finger continues it.'[1]

The first *tremblement* in our table, which is the one on *d'*, is done
by first unstopping the 6th hole, and blowing just as before so as
to play *e'*, which is the upper note. You give a tongue stroke on
this *e'* and beat several times on the 6th hole without retaking
breath, and without giving any more tongue strokes. Finally the
finger which has shaken must stay on the same hole to finish the
tremblement. The number of blows which you must give is regulated only by the value of the note.[2] Above all, it is necessary to
observe not to hurry in beating the *tremblement*, but, on the contrary,

[1] The *tremblement* is a trill with no turn or other ending. This is perhaps
because of the difficulties of fingering and tuning such an ending on the
instrument. He gives a turned trill called a *double cadence* in chapter 8. The trill
was sometimes notated // in England.
[2] Although in his introduction to the *Pieces pour la flûte* . . . *Livre Premier*,
he says that the speed of the *tremblement* is regulated by the tempo and
character of the piece.

to suspend it about half the value of the note, principally in slow movements, (as I show it in the table of *tremblements*).[1] The least number you should beat on short *tremblements* is three blows of the finger, as on crochets in fast 2 and 3 time.

It would be superfluous to explain all the *tremblements* one after the other, since you can see a demonstration in the second plate which is intelligible enough; and you must already know all the notes of which they are composed. For all these *tremblements* you should use the same rules that I have given for the first one; and should observe exactly the different positions of the fingers which you see demonstrated in the table.

I must only distinguish the *tremblement* on c'' natural, because it is in effect different from the others. You must begin it by stopping all the holes except the 1st; shake on the 4th, (after having sustained the *port-de-voix*) and finish by lifting the finger which has shaken. This is the opposite of what you observe in the other *tremblements*. With regard to the *tremblement* on c''', I must say that it is extremely difficult to adjust, and is very little in use. You can see from the table that the d''' which precedes it is done in an extraordinary way. You must shake on the 4th and 5th holes at the same time, and advance your finger a little on the 6th hole. You can also do this *tremblement* by shaking on the 3rd and 6th holes at the same time. Then all the holes must be stopped except the 1st; and you must lift up again the fingers which have shaken in finishing the *tremblement*. A *flattement* is often done on this note instead of a *tremblement*.

When you have learnt all the *tremblements* on the naturals, you could try to play some easy little Airs, to accustom yourself little by little to playing the notes, and to improve your embouchure. You

---

[1] i.e. the appoggiatura of the trill must be prolonged to half the value of the whole trill, particularly in slow movements. This rule is often forgotten by modern players. The reasons for the long appoggiatura are: (1) its function in making a discord; (2) the fact that it can be played in tune, even if the nature of the fingerings and tunings of the notes involved in the trill make it inevitable that the trill proper is not accurate. Thus the appoggiatura helped to persuade the ear that all was well. See, for example, the description of the e' flat/d' *tremblement* in chapter 6. For later examples of trill fingerings which are very much influenced by these of Hotteterre, see Corrette pp. 24–29, Quantz, chapter 9, and Mahaut pp. 11–18.

could even pass to this exercise as soon as you knew how to find the naturals of the first plate. In this case, it would be necessary to look for the *tremblements* in the second plate as you had to deal with them, which would burden your memory less. I give another explanation of *tremblements* in Chapter 6.

Chapter 5

Second explanation of the first plate (sharps and flats)

When you have improved your embouchure on the naturals, you could begin on the sharps and flats. But as there are several of these semitones which it is necessary to adjust by means of the embouchure, I am going to explain each one of them individually.

You should start on *d'* natural so as to link up the naturals with the sharps and flats, and to accustom your ear to appreciate the difference early on.

You should afterwards do *d'* sharp, by putting your little finger on the key to unstop the 7th hole.

e' and *f'* are produced as I have shown above in the explanation of the naturals. If you were to ask me why there is no sharp between these two notes, I would reply that it is because it is only a semitone from one to the other. For this reason, when a sharp is found on *e*, you use *f* natural, which has the ordinary effect of a sharp, viz. to raise the note by a semitone. You must remember to turn the mouth hole of the flute inwards, which must be done by lowering your head a little.

f' sharp is formed by unstopping the 6th and 7th holes, leaving the 5th unstopped as it has been already. I explain it in this way so that you know that you must not replace your fingers at each note, but must lift them immediately, as it is marked in the table. To adjust this note you must turn the flute outwards, and raise your head a little. By these terms, 'turn the flute' and 'turn the mouth hole', you must understand the same thing.

I will no longer explain the position of the fingers, for I suppose that you will presently know the table well enough to have need of no more explanation. I will discuss only the way of adjusting the notes.

As you have turned the flute outwards to adjust the *f'* sharp, it is necessary for you to replace it in its normal position for *g'* natural: after which you should do *g'* sharp, and turn the flute inwards to adjust it.

You should replace it in its normal position for *a'* natural, and turn it inwards again for *a'* sharp. You could otherwise lower this semitone by adjusting some fingers, which I have demonstrated in the plate of *tremblements*.[1]

You should replace it for *b'* and *c''* naturals. There is no sharp between these two notes, for the same reason that I gave when discussing *e'* and *f'*. You should therefore use *c''* natural to do *b'* sharp.

You should afterwards turn the flute outwards by as much as you can for *c''* sharp.

You should replace it for *d''* natural and sharp: and then immediately do *e''* and *f''* naturals. There is no semitone between these two notes, as I remarked in treating the low ones.

You should adjust *f''* sharp, *g''* natural and *g''* sharp, as I have demonstrated in discussing them an octave lower. I will explain another way of doing the last one in Chapter 7; but as this way is simpler, we will start by learning it.

You should replace the flute for *a''* natural, and turn it inwards for *a''* sharp.

You should replace it for *b''* and *c'''* naturals, and turn it outwards for *c'''* sharp. I will explain this semitone again in another way in Chapter 7.

You should replace the flute for *d'''* natural and sharp, unless they are not sufficiently low, as they are on some flutes. In this case it would always be necessary to turn the flute outwards. These high notes are difficult to adjust, and you must have a good ear, and practice.

You must also turn the mouth hole of the flute outwards for *e'''*, and sustain your breath well.

I have explained *f'''* sharp and *g'''* natural above, so it would be superfluous to discuss them again here. Let us, then, pass at once to the flats, which almost correspond to the sharps, except that

---

[1] i.e. 13456. (Also 134567.) The tone is a little more 'veiled' with this fingering.

what the flat does to a note the sharp does to the note below. This is for the reason that a flat lowers the note by a semitone, and a sharp raises it by a semitone. The *tremblements* on them are completely different, as you can see in the plate. (I will speak no longer about the naturals; but it will be good to do them immediately, as they are in the first plate; and to adjust them as I have explained above.)

You can therefore see from the table that *e'''* flat corresponds to *d'''* sharp.

d''' flat could also be produced like *c'''* sharp, but it is more perfect in the way in which I show it in the table.

b'' flat is formed like *a''* sharp. You must turn the flute outwards, which gives some difference between the *b* flat and *a* sharp.[1] It is necessary on some flutes to unstop the 7th hole to facilitate this note.

a'' flat is formed like *g''* sharp.

g'' flat could also be produced like *f''* sharp, but it is more perfect as I show it in the table. To adjust it you must turn the flute inwards a lot. This semitone is very little used, and is only met with in highly chromatic passages, which you scarcely compose for this instrument.[2]

e'' flat is fingered like *d''* sharp. You must turn the flute outwards a lot, in order to adjust this semitone.

b' flat like *a'* sharp.

---

[1] The fingering for *b''* flat of 124567 is shown in the trill tables. It was used in sequences such as *c''*/*b''* flat/*a''* flat according to Quantz.

There is some attempt on these notes and others later on, to bring out enharmonic distinctions by fingerings or by adjusting the embouchure differently. However, the distinctions are not consistent, e.g. '*b*' flat is done like *a'* sharp'. One can infer from his statement, 'several people do not make this difference', that in fact these enharmonic differences were only half-heartedly carried out.

It is interesting that the old English translation and *Modern Musick-Master* change over to tempered tuning, and the later tables in Corrette and Diderot also show this. Quantz made a great fuss on this matter—using different fingerings for virtually every enharmonic pair, and even introducing an extra key for *e''* flat (in addition to the existing one for *d''* sharp) in 1726 while he was in Paris. Perhaps it was listening to the best French flautists making these differences which finally convinced Quantz of the necessity for the second key.

[2] It is, however, found in Hotteterre's own preludes in *L'Art de Préluder*.

a' flat like *g'* sharp, but it is not necessary to turn the flute inwards as much. *g'* flat is different from *f'* sharp, like its octave. You must adjust it in the same way by turning the flute inwards. Several people do not make this difference.

e' flat like *d'* sharp.

When I compare a certain flat with a sharp, you should appreciate that the comparison is between two notes which are almost the same. For example, I said that *e'* flat is done like *d'* sharp, and so on for the others.

As regards the observations which I have made on the justness of the semitones, and turning the flute inwards or outwards; I will say that you must not hinder yourself with this delicacy at the beginning, or you should only do it roughly. You should content yourself with acquiring practice in the embouchure and fingering: after which you can exercise yourself on these refinements which are essential for perfection, and which you can only possess with time.

I have not shown *c'* sharp in my table, because this semitone is done only by artifice, having no special fingering.[1] You can do it like *d'*, by stopping all the holes, but turn the mouth hole of the flute inwards sufficiently to obtain a semitone. You can do the *tremblement* as for *d'*.

---

[1] It seems that as early as this people were trying to extend the compass of the flute downwards. Quantz, writing in 1752, remarks (Chapter 1, par. 16), 'About thirty years ago, several people wanted to add one more tone at the end, namely the C. Because of this they made the foot as much longer as was required for a whole tone, and another key was put on in order to have the C sharp. But because it appeared to be detrimental to correct tuning and the tone of the flute, this presumed invention disappeared again, and has not become general.' However, a trio sonata for two flutes and continuo by Fortunato Chelleri (probably written 1731-4) which Johannes Brinckmann found in a Swedish library has one of the flutes going down to this *c'*. In Majer's *Museum Musicum* of 1732 (p. 33), there is a picture and fingering chart of a flute going down to *c'*, with such an extra key. The middle joint of this flute is still in one piece. An extension down to *c'* sharp and *c'* become a standard fitting around 1800.

Chapter 6

Second explanation of the second plate
(tremblements *on sharps and flats*)

So that you can understand the signs on the musical notes, and on some of the O's of the table in the second plate, I will give an explanation of them here.

(1) The slur which joins the two notes of music, as here:

shows that it is only necessary to give one tongue stroke for the two notes. It is given on the first note (which only serves as preparation or *port-de-voix* to the *tremblement*) and you continue the same breath, without taking another one, up to the end of the *tremblement*: which I have already explained elsewhere. The little cross which is underneath signifies that it is on this note that you must shake.

(2) The stroke which joins the two O's of the table shows on which hole the *tremblement* starts, and on which it terminates. Through this you can see which are 'borrowed' *tremblements*, i.e. ones which do not end on the hole where you do the *port-de-voix*. For example, that on *d'* taken from *e'* flat, is started on *e'* flat by putting the little finger on the key, and is finished on the *e'* natural by shaking the 6th finger on the 6th hole, leaving the 7th restopped. You can also see a curly stroke on the second circle, to mark that it is on this hole that you must shake.

The *tremblement* on *e'* natural taken from *f'* sharp is of this kind. You begin it by unstopping the 5th, 6th and 7th holes to make the *f'* sharp (which serves it as a *port-de-voix*), and continue it by re-stopping the 5th and shaking on the 4th, which sharpens the higher note, and shows off the *tremblement* more highly: whereas by shaking on the 5th, it would not make enough effect. You must be careful to lift your little finger above the key again when you shake, (because otherwise the *e'* would be sharpened and rendered false)—which is shown by the table.

I will also give an explanation of the different effect of the sharps and flats on the natural *tremblements*. For example, *e'* flat and *d'* sharp are done in the same way, but you can see that the *tremblement* on *e'* flat is taken from *f'* natural; and that that on *d'* sharp is taken from *e'* natural: the first being of a whole tone, and the other of a semitone, which makes all the difference. It is the same with all the others.

You must take note that the *tremblements* or *cadences* are not always marked in pieces as I have described them here. Only the little cross is marked, in this way: +. There is nothing which indicates the *port-de-voix*, but you must not omit to do it, and to observe all that I have explained above.

There are some high notes where you cannot do *tremblements*. I have shown those which can be done, but you should note that those above *b''* are rarely practised.[1]

Furthermore I have not spoken of the way of adjusting the *tremblements*. This would only be a repetition of what I have already explained in mentioning the notes themselves, seeing that these *tremblements* are composed of the same notes. I will say only that there are some of them which you must commence by turning the mouth hole of the flute inwards, and finish by turning it outwards. Such is the *tremblement* on *f'* sharp taken from *g'* sharp; because the two notes which compose it must be adjusted differently. There are others where it is necessary to observe exactly the opposite, which you will know from the explanations which I have given on all these notes in Chapters 3 and 4.

With these explanations, and the demonstrations which you can see in the second plate, you could easily learn to do all the *tremblements*. There are some of them which are begun by stopping the

---

[1] Trills on *c'''*, *c'''* sharp, and *d'''* became fairly standard practice in the next twenty years.

hole on which you must shake, and which are finished by un-stopping this same hole. Such is the *tremblement* on c'', of which I have spoken in Chapter 4. You will know this difference by the arrangement of the circles, in which the black circle precedes the white circle; which is the opposite of the others.

Chapter 7

Remarks on some semitones, and on some tremblements

In order to omit nothing, I will now discuss some semitones and some *tremblements* which can be done in a different way from how I have shown them. I will commence with *g''* sharp which I have shown in my table in the simplest way. But as it is a little sharp in this first fashion, several means are used to make it flatter.

(i) After having stopped the 1st, 2nd and 4th holes (as you see it in the table), you stop the 6th hole as well, and unstop the 7th by means of the key. This way is sufficiently in use, and some people even do the *tremblement* with the 4th and 6th fingers at the same time; but it is not well articulated, as it is difficult for a *tremblement* done with two fingers thus separated from each other to be very distinct. I would advise you always to 'borrow' the *tremblement* with the 2nd finger, as I have shown it in the plate of *tremblements*; adjusting it by means of the embouchure, i.e. by turning the mouth hole of the flute inwards. You must also be careful not to lift your finger a lot in shaking.

(ii) You stop the 1st, 2nd and 4th holes, and afterwards half of the 5th, but with discretion. This way is a little better than the other one, because it uses only two fingers of the bottom hand, which, being neighbours, act with more facility. The *tremblement* is always taken from the 2nd finger, also turning the flute inwards. There are certain passages where you must play this semitone as I have demonstrated in the table, in order to avoid a great deal of difficulty.

What I have said about *g''* sharp also applies to *a''* flat, except the *tremblement* which is different, as you can see in the plate of *tremblements*.

The *tremblement* on *c'''* sharp can also be produced in several ways. I will give an explanation of them here, as well as of several others, rather to satisfy curiosity then to prescribe a frequent usage for them: for these *tremblements* cannot be done on all kinds of flutes with the same ease.

The first way is by stopping the 2nd and 3rd holes, and by shaking on the 4th and 6th at the same time. All the other holes must be unstopped, even the 7th. It is also necessary that the fingers which have shaken should stay on their holes in finishing the *tremblement*.

The second way is to stop all the holes except the 1st and 5th. You must shake on the 6th hole, and leave it unstopped in finishing the *tremblement*. Or else you can shake on the key and observe the same thing.

c''' sharp without *tremblement* can also be done by stopping the 3rd and 4th holes, leaving the others unstopped. *d'''* flat the same.

I will note in mentioning the *tremblement* on *b''* natural again, that you can do it by stopping the three holes of the bottom hand, and shake as usual on the 1st hole. It can be done easily in this way, but it is a little too sharp, and it is thus necessary to turn the mouth hole inwards to adjust it. That on *b''* flat can be made by half stopping the 2nd hole, and by shaking on the 1st and on the 3rd hole. Or else you can do it by shaking on the 1st and 3rd holes at the same time, leaving all the others unstopped. But it is not very natural in this way.

The *tremblement* on *a''* sharp can be produced by stopping all the holes except the 3rd and 7th. It is necessary to shake on the 2nd hole, and to turn the mouth hole of the flute inwards.

That on *d'''* natural taken from *e'''* flat, can also be formed on the 5th and 6th holes at the same time; keeping the first three stopped, and unstopping the 4th and 7th. You must force your breath and leave your fingers off in finishing the *tremblement*. There are some flutes where it is necessary to unstop the 1st hole.

I will say in mentioning *c''* natural again, that there are several people who do it by stopping the 2nd, 4th and 5th holes. But this way does not seem good to me, because in doing it in this way, it is not removed enough from its sharp, and the latter is not just.

Chapter 8

On the tongue strokes, ports-de-voix, accents *and* double cadences *on the flute and other instruments*

Now that I have explained the way of doing the tones and semitones with all their tremblements, it remains for me to discuss the tongue strokes[1] and ornaments which are absolutely necessary for perfection of playing. These ornaments consist of *ports-de-voix, accents, doubles cadences, flattements, battements,* etc. I will commence with an explanation of all the tongue strokes, both articulated and slurred, of which I will give several examples (as also of the *ports-de-voix, accents* and *doubles cadences*), which could be used for all wind instruments. Afterwards I will explain the way of doing *flattements* and *battements* on the flute.

To render playing more agreeable, and to avoid too much uniformity in the tongue strokes, you vary them in several ways. For example, two principal articulations namely *tu* and *ru*[2] are used. The *tu* is more common, and is used almost exclusively—on semibreves, minims, crochets, and on most quavers. For when these last are on the same line, or they leap, you pronounce *tu*[3]. When they ascend or descend by steps you also use *tu*, but you always intermix it with *ru*, as you can see in the examples below, where the two articulations succeed one another:

[1] As Betty Bang says in her article 'A Summer in Germany with a one-keyed flute' (*American Music Teacher*, April/May 1966), 'Unfortunately most twentieth century flutists have been either unaware of the complete explanations [of Hotteterre and Quantz] or they have not understood them. Without them much of the charm of the old music is lost'. For later discussions of tonguing see Quantz (Chapter 6) and Tromlitz (pp. 154–237).
[2] See my introduction for a discussion of the significance of these two syllables.
[3] This is not strictly true, for a permissible situation where both *tu* and *ru* can be used when quavers are on the same line is shown in the first example.

You must note that the *tu* and *ru* are ruled by the number of quavers. When the number is odd, you pronounce *tu ru* in succession, as in the first example. When it is even, you pronounce *tu* on the first two quavers, then alternate *ru* with it, as you see in the second example.

You will do well to note that you must not always play quavers equally, but that you must, in certain time signatures, make one of them long and one short; which is also ruled by their number.

When the number is even, you make the first one long, the second one short, and so on for the others. When it is odd, you do exactly the opposite: that is called 'pointing'. The time signatures in which this is most usually practised are 2 time, 3 time and ⁶₄ time.

You must pronounce *ru* on the note which follows the quaver, when it ascends or descends a step.

There are also certain time signatures where you only use *tu* for the quavers, e.g.

---

¹ This seems to be a mistake for 2 time: for Hotteterre later gives ₵ as one of the time signatures where *tu* only is used for the quavers.

You pronounce *tu* on all the quavers, and only use *ru* for the semi-quavers, i.e. the quavers correspond to crochets, and the semi-quavers to quavers, in this sort of time signature, as well as in $\frac{6}{8}$, $\frac{9}{8}$ and $\frac{12}{8}$ times. It is also necessary in these time signatures to take the quavers equally and 'point' the semiquavers.

You use *ru* on semiquavers following the rules which I have given previously for quavers. But you use it even more frequently, for even if the semiquavers are on the same line, or they leap, you must not neglect to do it e.g.

Although these rules are general, they do however admit some exceptions in certain passages, as you can see here:

[1] In the original *tururutu*, but altered in the facsimile Amsterdam edition, the old English translation and the *Modern Musick-Master* to this, which is presumably correct, for the original would contravene the rule, 'you should note . . . not to pronounce *ru* . . . on two successive notes'.

You understand that it is necessary to pronounce *tu* and *ru* on the first two quavers or semiquavers of even number, which is frequently practised when there are two quavers intermixed with crochets, or else two semiquavers with quavers. That is done for a greater sweetening or softening, and it is taste which decides it. You must consult this same taste when the tongue strokes seem harsh doing them in the way in which I have just explained them in the first examples. You must settle for whatever seems most agreeable to the ear, without having regard to the arrangement of the notes, or to the different time signatures. You should be careful only not to pronounce *ru* on *tremblements*; nor on two successive notes, for *ru* must always be alternated with *tu*.

In $\frac{3}{2}$ time you pronounce *tu* and *ru* on the crochets, and *ru* on a minim which is preceded by a crochet ascending or descending a step:-

We could thus put forward that all the triple times correspond to 3 time, and say that in $\frac{3}{2}$ time the minims correspond to crochets, and the crochets to quavers: which is why you must 'point' the crochets in this time signature, following the explanation which I have given on the subject of quavers previously.

It will be good to note that the tongue strokes must be more or less articulated, according to the instrument you play. For example, you soften them on the flute, you mark them more on the recorder, and you pronounce them a lot more strongly on the oboe.

On the Coulez

We must now pay attention to the *coulez*. These are two or several notes taken with the same tongue stroke; which is marked above or below the notes by slurs.[1]

[1] Notice that slurs are given the character of ornaments. Although *tu* is the only tongue stroke given to the *coulez* here, Hotteterre has a piece called 'Les Tourterelles' in his *Première Suite de Pièces à deux dessus* where the title is an imitation of the use of the articulation series *tuturu*—

It is important to note that inequality is used mostly without any slurring at all. Some people seem to think that pairs of notes to be played unequal must be written and/or played slurred. Hotteterre does not say that the marking of *coulez* affects inequality.

Betty Bang has kindly communicated to me the following personal opinions. Notes slurred in pairs which would normally be played unequal, are still played unequal, but may be done a little less so than usual. Three note slurs may be only slightly unequal. Groups of four or more notes under slurs probably should be played virtually or actually equal. It depends very much upon the context and the taste of the performer.

On the ports-de-voix *and* coulements[1]

The *port-de-voix* is a tongue stroke, anticipating the note on which you want to do it by a step from below. The *coulement* is taken a step above, and is rarely used except in descending intervals of thirds:

These little notes which mark the *ports-de-voix* and *coulements* are counted for nothing in the bar. Nevertheless, you articulate them and slur the principal notes to them. *Battements* are often joined to *ports-de-voix*, as you can see in the places marked in the examples of

---

[1] The *port-de-voix* is an ascending appoggiatura. It was called a 'sigh' in England. Hotteterre's wording is unclear as to how it should be played. It should not be assumed that because it is marked with a small crochet, its real length is a crochet. The phrase, 'these little notes . . . are counted for nothing in the bar' seems to indicate that the ornament was played very short. This interpretation is agreed with by his contemporaries in the flute world. Freillon-Poncein, who marks it by a small semiquaver, states, 'Ornaments are played very quickly on the same tongue stroke as the main note'. Corrette and Mahaut have to point out that the Italian appoggiatura must be played long, unlike its French counterpart. It is not clear whether Hotteterre means it to be played on or before the beat. Both interpretations were common at the time. If played weakly it is difficult to tell whether it is on or off the beat. Hotteterre also uses the sign V to indicate this ornament.

The *coulement* is a passing appoggiatura, which Hotteterre also indicates with a ʌ above the note. It was called a 'slide' in England. According to Quantz (Chapter 8, par. 6) it was played short and before the beat, e.g.

is played

64

ports-de-voix by a (3) and a (4). You will learn about *battements* in Chapter 9.

On accents *and* doubles cadences[1]

The *accent* is a sound which you 'borrow' from the end of some notes, in order to give them more expression. The *double cadence* is an ordinary *tremblement* followed by two semiquavers, slurred or articulated.

[1] The *accent* is a kind of passing appoggiatura, with whose interpretation Quantz agrees. It is often indicated by a ∣ instead of a small crochet. Corrette gives the following example, adding 'When this ornament is not marked you can do it on long notes when they descend by step, and also when there are several notes at the same pitch.'

The third example of the accent has been changed to *e″* in the facsimile Amsterdam edition. This is probably a mistake made when transposing the example from the French violin clef into the treble clef.

The *double cadence* is a turned trill, but note that the turn can be articulated. It is often indicated ∿ or + ⊃ when a short rest is made before the next note.

The *Modern Musick-Master* loses the whole point of this example, by missing out the trill signs and the slur!

Chapter 9

On *the* flattements *or minor* tremblements,
and the battements[1]

The *flattement* or minor *tremblement* is made almost like the ordinary *tremblement*. There is the difference that you always lift the finger off in finishing it, except on *d''*. You do it mostly on further removed holes, and some on the edge or extremity of holes. It shares the lower sound, which is the opposite of the *tremblement*.

The *battement* is produced by beating once or twice in succession, and as quickly as you can, full on the hole next to the one of the note you want to do it on. You must again take your finger off in finishing the *battement*, except on *d''*, as I will explain later. It also shares the lower sound.

To commence with the *flattement* on *d'* natural, following the order of the first plate, I will say that it can be done only by artifice. You cannot use any of your fingers for it (since they are all occupied in stopping the holes) so you shake the flute with your bottom hand, so that you can imitate the ordinary flattement by this means. You cannot have the *battement*.

The *flattement* on *d'* sharp or *e'* flat, is like that on *d'* natural. The *battement* is formed on the key with the little finger, which must remain there afterwards.

[1] The *flattement* is a fingered vibrato onto the flat side of the note in question. Normally nowadays vibrato is considered as being on both sides of a note, or onto the sharp side. Note that this ornament cannot be done on many notes on the modern Boehm flute. Quantz mentions this ornament in connection with the 'messa di voce' (a note held for half or a whole bar, with crescendo and decrescendo) in the chapter on the Adagio. It was called a 'softening' or 'lesser shake' in England and had the sign ⌇⌒ .

The *battement* is an inverted mordent. It was called a 'beat' in England and had the sign ' (which should not be confused with the identical French sign for the accent).

For further examples of *flattements* and *battements* see Corrette, pp. 30–33, and Mahaut p. 19. There are a few differences from here.

The *flattement* on *e'* natural is made on the edge of the 6th hole. The *battement* is formed on the whole of the same hole.

The *flattements* and *battements* on *f'* natural and sharp are made on the 5th hole; but the *flattements* on the edge of the hole, and the *battements* on the full hole.

The *flattement* on *g'* natural can be made in two ways: either on the edge of the 4th hole, or on the full 5th hole. The *battement* is made on the 4th hole.

The *flattement* on *g'* sharp or *a'* flat is formed on the edge of the 3rd hole. The *battement* on the same hole.

The *flattement* on *a'* natural on the 4th full hole, or on the edge of the 3rd. The *battement* on the 3rd.

The *flattement* on *a'* sharp or *b'* flat on the full 6th hole. The *battement* on the same hole, or on the 2nd when it is preceded by a port-de-voix.

The *flattement* on *b'* natural on the 3rd hole. The *battement* on the 2nd.

The *flattement* on *c''* natural on the 4th full hole. The *battement* on the 4th and 5th holes at the same time, or on the 1st when it is preceded by a *port-de-voix*.

The *flattement* on *c''* sharp or *d''* flat on the 2nd full hole.[1] The *battement* on the 1st.

The *flattement* on *d''* natural on the 2nd hole. It is different from the others, in that it is necessary to hold the hole stopped both in beginning and finishing it. You must take care not to raise your finger a lot. The *battement* is produced on the 4th hole when you play in a natural key: and on the 2nd and 3rd holes at the same time when you play in a key where *c* is sharpened. It is necessary that the holes also be stopped in beginning and ending.

The *flattement* on *d''* sharp or *e''* flat is formed on the 1st hole, which must remain stopped both before and afterwards. The *battement* is made on the key for the *e''* flat in the way which I have explained in discussing *e'* flat. When on the *d''* sharp it is done on the 2nd and 3rd holes at the same time. The 1st hole must be un-

---

[1] Corrette remarks, 'The *anciens* did it on the 2nd hole, but it is worthless and lowers the note by a comma', and advocates use of the 3rd full hole.

stopped, and it is necessary to restop the 2nd and 3rd holes in finishing the *battement*.

The *flattements* and *battements* after this note, up to *a''* sharp or *b''* flat, are made like their octaves. The *flattement* of this latter is formed on the edge of the 4th hole. The *battement* can be produced on the same hole, or else on the 2nd, principally when it is preceded by a *port-de-voix*.[1]

The *flattement* on *c'''* natural is formed in two ways: viz. either on the 6th hole or on the 3rd. The *battement* the same, and also on the 1st hole when it is preceded by a *port-de-voix*.[2]

The *flattement* on *d'''* natural on the 2nd hole like that on its octave. The *battement* on the 2nd and 3rd holes at the same time.

The *flattement* on *d'''* sharp or *e'''* flat is also formed like its octave. The *battement* the same, or else on the 5th and 6th holes at the same time. You must keep the 4th and 7th unstopped. You must replace the fingers in finishing.

The *flattement* on *e'''* natural on the edge of the 3rd hole. The *battement* on the same full hole.

I will leave the notes above these, as they are too forced. It would even only be necessary to do some of these last when you are extremely advanced.

These ornaments are not marked in all pieces of music, and are only normally in those which teachers write for their pupils. Here is the way:

Furthermore, it would be difficult to teach precise knowledge of all the situations in which you must place them in playing. What you can add to this in general is that *flattements* are frequently made on

---

[1] The *flattement* and *battement* on *b''* are not given. Mahaut gives the edge of the 3rd hole or the full 4th hole for the *flattement*: Corrette gives the 2nd hole for the *battement*.

[2] The *flattement* and *battement* on *c'''* sharp or *d'''* flat are not given. Mahaut gives the edge of the 5th hole or the full 6th hole for the *flattement*: Corrette gives the 5th hole for the *battement*.

[3] This ornament is missed out in the facsimile of the Amsterdam edition.

long notes: as on semibreves A, on minims B, on dotted crochets C, etc. The *battements* are made more commonly on short notes: as on crochets D in fast movements, and on quavers in time signatures where they are taken equally. You can scarcely give more certain rules on the distribution of these ornaments: it is taste and practice which can teach their appropriate use, rather than theory. What I can advise is for you to play for some time on pieces where all the ornaments are marked: and then to accustom yourself little by little to doing them on the notes where they turn out best.

END OF THE TREATISE ON THE FLUTE

TREATISE ON THE
RECORDER

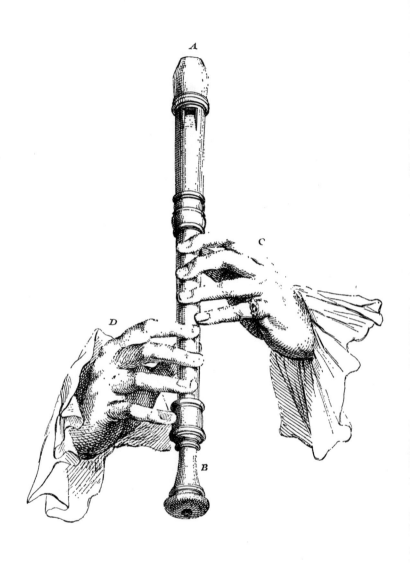

Chapter 1

On the situation of the recorder and the position of the hands

The recorder having its merits and its partisans just like the flute, I believed that it would not be completely useless to give here a little treatise especially for it.

I will commence with an explanation of the way in which you must hold the recorder, and of the position in which your hands must be; which you can already see represented in the above picture.

(1) You must hold the recorder straight in front of you; and place the high end A (called the beak) between your lips, as little forward as you can. The low end B (called the foot) must be about a foot in distance from your body, so that you can place your hands on top of the recorder without constraining them. You should not raise your elbows, but let them fall loosely near your body.

(2) You should place your left hand C on top and your right hand D below, as you see demonstrated. The thumb of your left hand must stop the hole which is underneath the recorder, and which is the highest of them. I will call this the 1st hole, the one after it the 2nd hole, and so on for the others in descending order. The thumb of your right hand must be placed under the recorder, opposite the finger on the 5th hole, or a little lower down. This thumb serves only to support the recorder. You must, as far as you can, hold *all* your fingers straight, but principally those of the bottom hand: and accustom the little finger of this hand to stop the 8th hole little by little. This is a bit difficult at the beginning.

You must not stop the holes with the tips of your fingers, but advance them on the recorder, so that the end of each finger passes over the end of its hole by about one third or one quarter of an inch. As the middle finger of each hand is longer than the others, it must be bent a little, so that it falls more exactly on the hole, and you have more facility for stopping the hole.

73

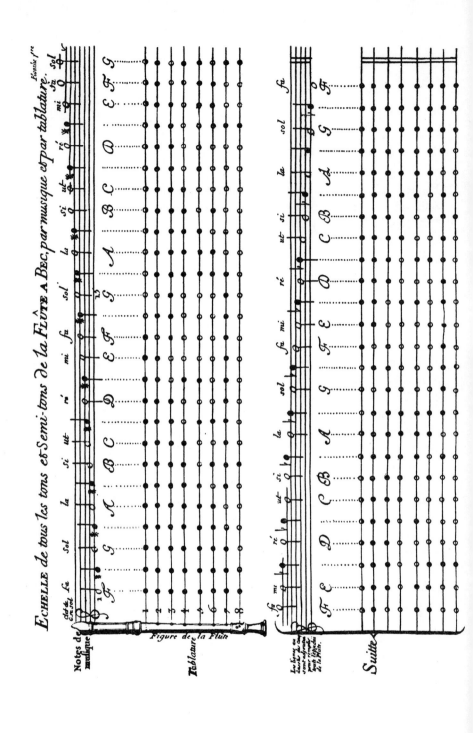

Echelle de tous les tons et Semi-tons de la FLUTE A BEC, par musique et par tablature.

Planche 1.re

Figure de la Flûte

Notes de musique

Tablature

Suitte

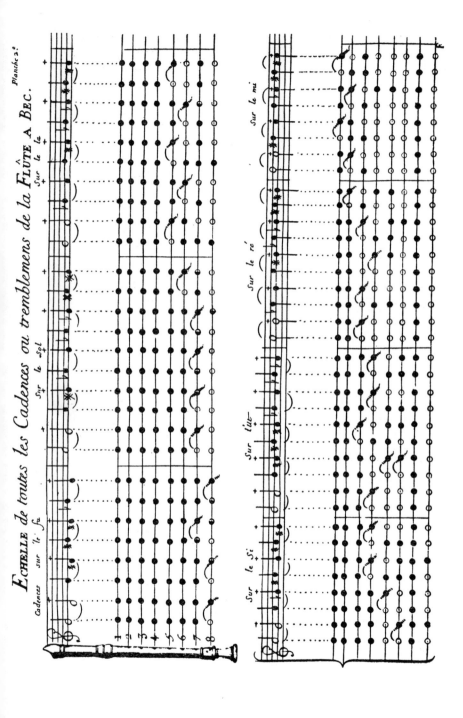

ECHELLE de toutes les Cadences ou tremblemens de la FLUTE A BEC.

Planche 2.

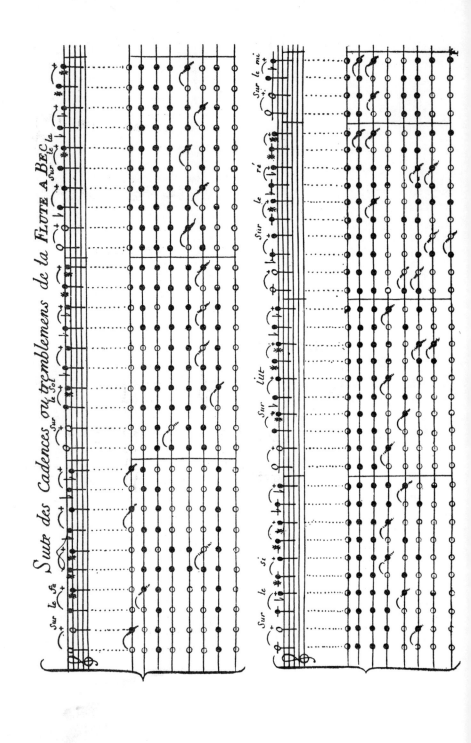

Suite des Cadences ou tremblemens de la FLUTE A BEC

Chapter 2

Explanation of the first plate (all the notes)

I will here use a table similar to that which you can see in the treatise on the flute, so it would be superfluous to give a second explanation of it. Those then who want to begin with the recorder, should run through Chapter 3 of the treatise of which I have just spoken. They could instruct themselves sufficiently in the knowledge of this table there, as well as in the notes of music. But for those people it will be necessary to change some positions of the explanations, so as to make then conform completely to the plate of recorder tones and semitones. For example, you see that there are eight holes on the recorder, and that there are only seven on the flute. You also see that the first note of the recorder is f', whereas that of the flute is d'. You should thus make this distinction in reading this third chapter, and should say in the appropriate place, 'This table is demonstrated by the eight parallel lines which correspond to the eight holes of the recorder'; and a little lower down, 'Below the first note, which is f'', you see eight circles on the perpendicular line described by the little dots. It is easy to understand that this represents the eight holes of the recorder stopped (the first four with the top hand, and the four others with the bottom hand): which gives this note'.

You should follow up to where the two different octaves are mentioned, where you should now make this change: 'It is only the "pinch" which makes the difference between them'.

You should continue up to where the explanation of the notes commences, and where we will leave that chapter to take it up here.

You see then from the table of the first plate, that to produce the note f' it is necessary to stop all the holes. You must also give a tongue stroke in blowing, as I have explained in Chapter 3 of the treatise on the flute. But the difficulty is to stop these eight holes well; because if the least air is lost, this note cannot be obtained. The difficulty arises partly from the little finger, which you have a lot of trouble at the beginning keeping away from the others, so that the eighth hole can be stopped. Thus it will be necessary to start with *g'*. You will find it easier, and it is also more in usage. However, to follow things in order, I will discuss *f'* sharp. This is produced by unstopping the middle of the 8th hole on recorders which do not have a double hole. But on those which have one[1] you unstop the further of these two holes, which you do by drawing back your finger without lifting it. You must only give a small amount of breath to the low notes, and augment it little by little in proportion as you ascend.

g' natural by unstopping the 8th hole completely.

g' sharp by unstopping half of the 7th hole, as I have explained in discussing *f'* sharp, or, if this is double, the further hole.

a' natural by unstopping the 7th hole completely without replacing anything.

a' sharp by unstopping the 6th hole and restopping the 7th.

b' natural by unstopping the 5th hole and stopping all the others.

c'' natural by unstopping the 6th and 8th holes, leaving the finger which was already on the 7th. This hole must be stopped almost always, as you see in the table.[2] There is no sharp from *b'*

[1] This is the only tutor outside modern times to mention these double holes on the 7th and 8th finger holes. But Hotteterre knew his subject and, as Edgar Hunt remarks (p. 52) 'Is it not strange that more specimens of eighteenth century recorders with these double holes have not survived? The present writer can recall only the examples by Bressan in the museums of Chester and Vienna, and another instrument at Stockholm.'

It seems probable that Bressan came to England from France in 1683, according to research done by Eric Halfpenny. Perhaps Hotteterre knew of these extra holes because of specimens Bressan left behind in France.

[2] This is the so-called *Stützfingertechnik* (supporting- or buttress-finger technique). Edgar Hunt comments (p. 108). 'The idea was to provide some extra support for the instrument by adding the 3rd finger of the right hand for some notes. The disadvantage is that the player has to remember *which* notes, and ensure that the extra finger does not spoil a note for which it is not required! Besides, the 3rd is supposed to be a weak finger, and this use of it is cramping to the hand-position. Instead, the writer advises the use of the 4th finger, which, when not otherwise occupied in closing the lowest hole, can rest on the beading between the two lowest holes. This corresponds to the use of the same finger on the D sharp key of the flute—an essential part of [modern Boehm] flute technique. It not only gives support, but helps in the

to *c''*, the reason being that there is only a semitone between these two notes. This is why you use *c''* natural to do *b'* sharp.

c'' sharp by unstopping the 4th hole, restopping the 5th and 6th.

d'' natural by unstopping the 5th and 6th holes, without changing any of the others.

d'' sharp by unstopping the 3rd hole and restopping the 4th and 5th.

e'' natural by unstopping the 4th and 5th holes without changing anything else.

f'' natural by unstopping the 2nd hole, and restopping the 3rd. This hole must remain stopped almost always. There is no sharp between *e* and *f* for the same reason I have already explained in mentioning *b'* and *c''*. You therefore use *f''* natural to do *e''* sharp.

f'' sharp by unstopping the 1st hole (the thumb hole) and restopping the 2nd hole.

g'' natural by unstopping the 2nd hole without changing anything else.

g'' sharp by stopping all the holes except the 1st and 8th.

a'' natural by unstopping the 7th hole without changing anything else. You must augment your breath a little here, so as to render the sound of the recorder sharp. Or else you can do this note by 'pinching', i.e. by making your nail enter into the thumb hole, so as to divide it in half. This is practised for all the high notes, as you can see in the table by the half-filled circles.

a'' sharp by unstopping the 6th hole and restopping half of the 7th. It is necessary to pinch it, as well as the following notes.

b'' natural by unstopping the 5th and 7th holes, and restopping the 6th.

c''' natural by unstopping the 6th hole, which means raising all the bottom hand.

c''' sharp by unstopping the 4th hole and restopping the 5th. It is necessary to moderate your breath. There are some recorders

---

location of the right-hand fingers after a passage in which they have not been involved.'

Hunt's method is similar to the one advocated for the flute by Hotteterre in Chapter 1. This is the main difference in fingering from the accepted modern ones.

which have this 4th hole double.[1] Then you half unstop it, and do not stop the 5th.

d''' natural by unstopping the 4th hole and lifting all the bottom hand.

d''' sharp by stopping the 6th, 7th and 8th holes, without changing any of the others. You can keep the 8th hole unstopped on some recorders.

e''' natural by unstopping the 7th and 8th holes, and stopping the 5th and 6th, without changing anything of the top hand.

f''' natural by unstopping the 3rd hole without changing anything else. There is no *f'''* sharp.

g''' natural by unstopping the 3rd and 6th holes, and stopping all the others. You must blow sharply.

When you have run through these notes I suppose you know the table enough to run through those which remain, which are the flats. You should find them easier in as much as they all correspond to the sharps,[2] as you can see in the table; except that what serves for the sharp on one note, serves for the flat on another—which I have already explained in Chapter 5 of the treatise on the flute. Thus I will not give another explanation of it, and will only discuss *e'* sharp, which I have not demonstrated in the table, because it is nothing but *f'* natural, as I have remarked in mentioning the high note. I also advise beginners at first to strive to produce only the naturals (distinguished by minims) in order to avoid a lot of difficulty.

[1] This is the answer to Edgar Hunt's puzzle. He shows a photograph of a Bressan recorder from the Kunsthistorisches Museum in Vienna, with just such double holes. He writes (p. 101), 'What can be the purpose of this? The writer has made experiments with a recorder of similar construction, but these have so far been inconclusive, though the device does make the high D-E trill easier. A similar double hole was usual on oboes of the eighteenth century for the two G sharps and the high D sharp.' This last statement in fact gives the clue to the true purpose of this double hole, for *g''* sharp on the oboe corresponds to *c'''* sharp on the treble recorder.

[2] It is interesting that no enharmonic differences are made for the recorder, c.f. the flute.

Chapter 3

Explanation of the tremblements

After you have learnt the naturals, you could learn to form the *tremblements* on these same notes; and for that you should run through the 4th and 6th chapters of the treatise on the flute, in which you will find an ample explanation of the *tremblement,* which will serve as instruction for those of the recorder, which are demonstrated in the second plate.

I will only then treat some *tremblements* in particular in this chapter, which will suffice for your understanding of all in general. I will commence with the one on *f'* natural, which is the first note of the same plate. You see from the table that the 8th hole is unstopped to start this *tremblement,* and must afterwards be stopped to finish it. You have seen in the treatise on the flute that you must beat several times, stopping the hole on which the *tremblement* ends. You should therefore do the same thing on all the others.

f' sharp is shaken like *f'* natural, except that you only stop half of the 8th hole in shaking. If the hole is double, you shake on the nearer of the two holes, which you do by drawing your finger back.

The *tremblement* on *f'* sharp taken from *g'* sharp is produced by first unstopping half of the 7th hole, stopping half of the 8th without changing anything, and shaking on the full 7th hole. These three movements must be done one after the other, and with only one tongue stroke: but this *tremblement* is little used.

That of *f'* natural taken from *g'* flat is found by first unstopping half of the 8th hole, and shaking on the same full hole. This *tremblement* also serves for *e'* sharp.

The explanation of these four *tremblements* must suffice to give understanding of all the others, with the help of the table. I will only speak of that on *g''* natural, because it is produced in a different way from the others. You prepare it with *a''*, but only by stopping the 3rd, 4th, 5th and 6th holes, after which you shake on the 4th, which must remain unstopped to finish. That is demonstrated by the open O, on which the curly stroke is placed. There are still others of the same kind; and also some which are done with two fingers at once, which you see demonstrated in the table by two curly strokes on the two circles one above the other.

It now only remains for us to discuss the *flattements* and *battements*, of which you will find an explanation in the next chapter. For the tongue strokes, *coulez, ports-de-voix, accents*, etc., you should read the 8th chapter of the treatise on the flute, where they are explained amply enough.

Chapter 4

On the flattements *and* battements

I have explained in chapter 9 of the treatise on the flute what the *flattement* and *battement* are, and the way of doing both of them. You should thus read the beginning of that chapter before reading this one: after which you should read the following explanations of the way to apply its precepts to the recorder.

To commence with the *flattement* on *f'* natural (always following the order of the first plate), I must say it can only be done by shaking the recorder with the bottom hand, as I explained for the first note of the flute. It is the same with *f'* sharp or *g'* flat. You cannot do the *battement* on these notes.

The *flattements* on *g'* natural, *g'* sharp and *a'* flat are produced on the edge of the 8th hole. The *battements* on the same notes on the same full hole.

The *flattement* on *a'* natural on the edge of the 7th hole. The *battement* on the whole of the same hole.

The *flattement* on *a'* sharp or *b'* flat is formed on the edge of the 6th hole. It can also be done on the 8th. The *battement* on the 6th full hole.

The *flattement* on *b'* natural is formed on the edge of the 5th hole. The *battement* on the same full hole.

The *flattement* on *c''* natural on half of the 5th or 6th hole. The *battement* is formed on this last full hole when you play in a natural key: and on the 5th when you play in a key where *b* is flat.

The *flattement* on *c''* sharp or *d''* flat is formed on the edge of the 4th hole, and the *battement* on the same hole.

The *flattement* on *d''* natural on the 5th full hole. The *battement* on the 4th, or else on the 5th and 6th when it is preceded by a sharp *port-de-voix*.

The *flattement* on *d''* sharp or *e''* flat on half of the 6th hole. The *battement* on the same full hole, or on the 3rd when preceded by a *port-de-voix*.

The *flattement* on *e''* natural on the 4th hole. The *battement* on the 3rd, or on the 4th when it is preceded by a *d''* sharp.

The *flattement* on *f''* natural is formed on the 5th full hole, or on half of the 4th. The *battement* on the 2nd or on the 4th.

The *flattement* on *f''* sharp or *g''* flat like that on *f''* natural. The *battement* on the 4th full hole, or on the 1st when it is preceded by a *port-de-voix*.

The *flattement* on *g''* natural is formed on the 4th full hole. The *battement* on the 2nd, or on the 1st when it is preceded by a natural *port-de-voix*.

The *flattement* on *g''* sharp or *a''* flat is formed on half of the 8th hole. The *battement* on the same hole, or on the 6th, unstopping the 3rd, and sometimes also the 2nd. In this case you must restop the hole in finishing, which is not done for the others.

The *flattement* on *a''* natural is formed on the edge of the 7th hole. The *battement* on the same full hole, but when it is preceded by a natural *port-de-voix* on the 4th hole, the 1st and 2nd being unstopped. You must again restop the hole in finishing.

The *flattement* on *a''* sharp or *b''* flat on the edge of the 6th hole. The *battement* on the same full hole.

The *flattement* on *b''* natural is formed on the edge of the 5th hole. The *battement* on the same full hole.

The *flattement* on *c'''* natural on the edge of the 5th or 6th hole. The *battement* on one of these two full holes.

The *flattement* on *c'''* sharp or *d'''* flat is formed on the edge of the 6th or the 4th hole. The *battement* on the 4th full hole.

The *flattement* on *d'''* natural on the edge of the 5th hole. The *battement* on the 4th hole, or on the 5th when it is preceded by a sharp *port-de-voix*.

The *flattement* on *d'''* sharp or *e'''* flat is formed on the edge of the 4th hole. The *battement* on the same full hole.

The *flattement* on *e'''* natural on half of the 7th hole. The *battement* on the same full hole, or on the 5th and 6th at the same time when it is preceded by a natural *port-de-voix*.

The *flattement* on *f'''* natural is formed on the 7th full hole. The *battement* on the 3rd.

The *flattement* on *g'''* on the 6th hole. The *battement* on the same.

END OF THE TREATISE ON THE RECORDER

Method for learning to play the oboe

The oboe is so related to the flute in the way of fingering the notes, that you could easily learn to play it by using the same principles.[1] These instruments only differ (with regard to the arrangement of the fingers) in some few notes. This difference is so small, that you will be perfectly instructed by reading the following explanations.

Explanation of the way of holding the oboe

You must hold the oboe almost like the recorder, with the difference that it must be a little more raised. In consequence you should hold your head erect, and your hands high; you should place them in the order that I explained in discussing the recorder, i.e. the left hand on top, the right below, etc.

Explanation of the embouchure

As regards the embouchure, you must place the reed[2] between your lips, exactly in the middle. You only push it into your mouth one-sixth or quarter of an inch, so that it is about an eighth of an inch from your lips to the wire of the reed. You should place it so that you can squeeze it more or less, as required, and should not touch it with your teeth.

Explanation of the naturals

The naturals are done as demonstrated in the first plate of the

[1] However, note what Quantz has to say on a similar subject (Chapter 2, par. 12): 'As the fingering of the flute has many similarities to that of the oboe, many suppose that someone who plays the oboe can learn the flute himself: and from this fallacy comes so much incorrect fingering, and unskilful type of embouchure.'
[2] An excellent discussion of contemporary reeds, and indeed the baroque oboe generally, is given by Phillip Bate in his book The Oboe (Ernest Benn).

treatise on the flute and as explained in the 3rd chapter of the same treatise, with the exception of *c'''* and *c''*, which are done in a different way. *c''* is done by stopping the 2nd hole (counting the holes like those on the flute), leaving all the others unstopped. The *tremblement* is done as on the flute, except that you must shake on the 3rd hole. (See the treatise on the flute, chapter 4). *c'''* is done by unstopping all the holes, or else by unstopping only the first three and stopping the 4th, 5th and 6th. There is one more C, *c'*, which is not shown in the table, because it is below the range of the flute. It is done by stopping all the holes and by supporting the little finger on the large key at the bottom on the oboe. It is shaken on this same key. You must note that you rarely ascend higher than *d'''*. You should observe also to augment your breath little by little in ascending, and to squeeze the reed with your lips.

Explanation of the sharps and flats

The sharps and flats are also done in conformity to the table of the flute, except for some of them which I am going to explain.

g' flat is formed by unstopping the 5th hole completely, and also half of the 4th; and by stopping all the other holes, except that of the large key. It is shaken on the 3rd hole. *f'* sharp is sometimes produced in the same way, and is shaken on half of the 4th hole, but it is more usually formed as on the flute. *g''* flat is formed by stopping all the holes, except the 4th and that of the large key. It is also shaken on the 3rd hole. *f''* sharp in the same way, and is shaken on the 5th hole. It is also produced as on the flute.

g' and *g''* sharps, *a'* and *a''* flats are all formed by unstopping half of the 3rd hole, by stopping the 1st and 2nd completely, and unstopping all the others. The *g* sharps are shaken on half of the 3rd hole, and the *a* flats on the 2nd hole.

The *a* sharps and *b* flats by stopping the 1st and 3rd holes, leaving all the others unstopped.

c'' sharp or *d''* flat is formed by unstopping the 1st hole, and stopping all the others, even that of the large key. *c''* sharp is shaken on the key with the little finger. *d''* flat is shaken with the 6th finger, all the holes being stopped: or else as on the flute. This semitone is also done at the octave above by forcing the breath and squeezing the reed with the lips.

With regard to the *tremblements,* tongue strokes, *flattements,* etc., you should read the explanations which I have given on these ornaments in the treatise on the flute.

If, in spite of the care I have taken to make these principles understandable, anyone should find any difficulties in them; I will always be pleased and honoured to clear them up for them, where I live at rue Christine, in Monsieur Royer's house.

Bibliography

Betty Bang: 'A summer in Germany with a one-keyed flute', *American Music Teacher,* April/May 1966.
Michel Corrette: *Méthode pour apprendre aisément à jouer de la flûte traversière,* Boivin and Le Clerc, Paris, Bretonne, Lyon. n.d.
Encyclopédie: edited by Diderot and d'Alembert. Vol. 6, Paris, 1756, articles 'Flûte Allemande ou Traversière' and 'Flûte à bec ou flûte douce'.
F. J. Fétis: *Biographie Universelle des Musiciens,* 2nd edn., Paris, 1883.
H. Macaulay Fitzgibbon: 'Of soft flutes and recorders', *Musical Quarterly,* 1934, p. 222.
Eric Halfpenny: 'A French Commentary on Quantz', *Music and Letters,* 1956, pp. 61–66.
Edgar Hunt: *The Recorder and its Music,* Herbert Jenkins, London, 1962.
Antonio Mahaut: *Nieuwe manier om binnen korten tyd op de dwarsfluit te leeren speelen* (with parallel French text, *Nouvelle méthode pour apprendre en peu de temps à jouer de la flûte traversière*), Amsterdam, J. J. Hummel, c. 1759.
J. F. C. B. Majer: *Museum Musicum Theoretico Practicum,* 1732. Facsimile Bärenreiter/Kassel, 1954.
The Modern Musick-Master, facsimile edn. Bärenreiter/Kassel. Flute section published separately as *The Newest Method for Learners on the German Flute.*
Eberhard Preussner: *Die Musikalischen Reisen des Herrn v. Uffenbach,* Bärenreiter/Kassel, 1949.
Johann Joachim Quantz: *Versuch einer Anweisung die Flöte traversière zu spielen.* Berlin, 1752. Facsimile of 3rd edn. of 1789 published by Bärenreiter/Kassel. English translation by E. R. Reilly as *On the Flute,* Faber, London, 1966.
Hans-Peter Schmitz: *Querflöte und Querflötenspiel in Deutschland während des Barockzeitalters,* Bärenreiter, Kassel, 2nd edition, 1958.
Ernest Thoinan: *Les Hotteterre et les Chédville, célèbres joueurs et facteurs de flûtes, hautbois, bassons et musettes des XVIIe et XVIIIe siècles,* Paris, 1894.
J. G. Tromlitz: *Ausführlicher und gründlicher Unterricht die Flöte zu spielen,* Leipzig, 1791.